Moving into Ecstasy

An urban mystic's guide to movement, music and meditation

Moving into Ecstasy

*An urban mystic's guide to movement,
music and meditation*

Amoda

Thorsons

Thorsons
An Imprint of HarperCollins*Publishers*
77–85 Fulham Palace Road
Hammersmith
London W6 8JB

The Thorsons website address is: www.thorsons.com

and *Thorsons* are trademarks of HarperCollins*Publishers* Limited

Published by Thorsons 2001

10 9 8 7 6 5 4 3 2 1

© Amoda 2001

Amoda asserts the moral right to be identified as the author of this work

A catalogue record for this book is available from the British Library

ISBN 0 00 711654 3

Text illustrations by Jane Spencer

Printed and bound in Great Britain by
Scotprint Limited, Haddington, East Lothian

For everyone who has ever found ecstasy on the dance-floor.

About the author

Amoda is a writer, teacher and healer. Her background is in psychology, rebirthing, Tantra, Shamanism and meditation. She has also been involved in the UK dance and music scene. She has published work in scientific journals and written numerous magazine articles. More recently, she has developed her own teaching method, 'Moving into Ecstasy', and runs classes, workshops and training.

Details can be found at **www.movingcreations.com** or you can e-mail **info@movingcreations.com**

Acknowledgements

From the first seeds that were planted as an idea in my mind to the final flowering that manifests as this book in your hands, there has been a web of magic created by all those who somehow have been a part of this journey – my appreciation and love go out to you all.

Thank you …

Victoria McCulloch, friend, assistant, advisor, fellow trance-dancer and sister on the path, for your gentle but insistent nudging to write this book in the first place, for your constant encouragement and feedback, for being a first-rate 'midwife' throughout the birth of this project … may we share many more journeys!

Belinda Budge, Publishing Director at Thorsons, for your role when this all started – your vision and enthusiasm fired me up to go ahead with it!
Louise McNamara, my commissioning editor at Thorsons, for your softly spoken smooth-sailing support which has cradled this book from inception to manifestation. The team at Thorsons for your work behind the scenes to make any of this possible, especially **Helen Evans** and **Vikki Renner.**

Michael Alcock and **Cathy Fischgrund,** my agents, for believing in me and for your speed of action – you really made this happen!

Ananda (or Nandi), Olli, Lizzi, Froggi and **Solli** for your absolute generosity in providing a safe shelter out there in the hills, for allowing me the space to shut myself away day after day to pour out page after page, for the fun and frolics when I needed a break … I honestly couldn't have done it without you!

The wonderful team of musicians I have come to know and work with – **Pragito** for your sensitivity and excellence of musical skills, **Satyaloka** for the steadfastness of your drum and the genius of your computer designs, and **Bob (the Shaman)** for your ability to move between the worlds without fear. I thank all of you for the generosity of your spirit and your support of my vision.

Everyone who has ever come to my classes and workshops, who has danced with me and shared a little bit of their story … you know who you are!

Stephen Russell (aka Barefoot Doctor) for being one step ahead on the 'hero's path' – it's good to know you!

Simon Buxton of the Sacred Trust for being a kindred spirit (and all the entertaining e-mails!)

Everyone around the world who has been a teacher in some form or another, who has inspired me, instructed me and assisted me to evolve as a human being. Most of all to **Osho**, the 'spiritually incorrect mystic', whose ever-lasting presence has made itself felt deep in my heart.

My Spirit Teachers – **White Eagle, Wise Owl, Sparrow-Hawkess** and **BlueJay (aka The Council of Four)**, for your wise counsel when the road got rocky (and the entertaining inner visions!).

Bagwan (the Orange Cat), the 'master of masters' – for reminding me just to 'be' (and for endless cuddles and dribbles!).

And last but certainly not least, **Jon Hall (aka Mr Lion)**, for being a witness to my endless transformations, for being a mirror for my growth, and for being my soul-mate – whether you like that role or not!

Contents

1: The Beginning

'The only joy in the world is to begin.'

CESARE PAVESE

The Beginning

Chapter 1

Wake Up!

Something could happen at any moment, and if you are not absolutely awake, absolutely still, you will miss it.

ECKHART TOLLE

An Invitation to Freedom

We all do it. We all get out of our heads. We do it when we fall in love and lose ourselves. We do it at the peak of a mind-blowing orgasm. Some of us do it wearing Nikes, mindlessly pounding the pavement mile after mile, until the world stops turning and we disappear into infinity. Sometimes we just do it watching the sun set on an endless horizon, so still and silent that time stretches into eternity.

Getting out of our heads is as natural as breathing. It is a part of being human. Most of us did it when we were little, spinning round and round until we fell into a heap on the floor. We didn't think to question why we did it. It just felt good. Feeling good, getting high, letting go – millions of people do it every weekend, mostly with the help of a variety of chemical intoxicants. 'Getting out of it' is second nature.

The desire to get out of our heads is a longing for freedom. Most of us, at some time or another, get a sense of being trapped. We are trapped by the humdrum of day-to-day tasks. We are trapped by the chains of material security. We are trapped by the voices of self-criticism that echo round in our heads. Deep in our souls we long for freedom. We are trapped chasing our own tails, for there is never enough time or money. But if we make time to take time-out from the self-imposed (because ultimately we always have a choice) Rules and Regulations of Life on Earth, we can start to see beyond the limitations of 'normal' life. By escaping the confines of our everyday, ordinary reality, we can rise above the incessant chatter inside our heads and see reality from a higher perspective.

Getting out of our heads is a doorway to something greater than ourselves. It is a glimpse of freedom, where for a moment (or longer if we are lucky!) time stands still, thoughts disappear and we transcend the 'thinking self'. It is in this moment that we awaken to who we really are, to the glory of our being and to the wonder of life as it is. In this moment, everything is perfect and we are free.

The quest for expanded states of consciousness is as old as humanity. Forty-thousand years ago, pre-historic matriarchal cultures sought ways to connect with a force greater than themselves. By dancing themselves into ecstasy and sometimes by ingesting plant-based substances, these people transcended mundane reality and experienced the magical world of the sacred. Remnants of these ancient practices survive to this day within indigenous tribes, such as the Yoruba of Africa, the Umbanda of Brazil and the Huichol of Mexico.

The quest continues in the East, where the *yogis* of traditional India follow arduous physical disciplines, such as not eating, not sleeping and hardly breathing, in order to transcend the limitations of the physical world. Conversely, the *dakinis* of Tibetan Buddhism and the *tantrikas* of Hinduism enter the world of the divine through the realm of the senses, using sexual practices for enlightenment. It is clear that the search for meaning is deeply embedded in our souls.

Today, most of us have lost this ability to bridge the physical and spiritual worlds and so our lives are less meaningful. Life has become one-dimensional, shortsighted, lacking in depth. In a world geared towards ever-increasing mechanization, urbanization and complication, we are increasingly forced to 'think quick', 'plan ahead', 'stay on top of things'. In this fast-paced world, we race against the tick-tock of time, striving to **do** more and more, forgetting that we are human **beings**. Bombarded by a smorgasbord of sensory stimulation, we live mainly in our heads, cut off from the rest of ourselves. We see the world through the myopic lens of our thinking brains and believe that this is all there is to life.

In our man-made world, we are out of touch with ourselves and out of touch with reality. Living in an artificial jungle, we are far removed from the pulse of life. Concrete walkways, high-rise buildings and 24-hour lighting insulate us from the natural vibrations of the Earth. Mobile phones, computer screens, TVs, stereos and advertising billboards drown out the subtle messages of our innate intelligence. Surrounded by the busy-ness of the modern urban world, we no longer feel the rhythm of Existence. We no longer sense the majesty of the cycles of Nature and we no longer hear the gentle but insistent voice of our inner nature.

Disconnected from our archaic roots, many of us feel lost and alone. We go about our daily business, trapped in the dialogue with our minds. We are like zombies, sleep-walking from one task to the next. In the rush forwards to advance technologically, we have forgotten who we really are. Disenchanted with the superficial pleasures of civilized society, more and more people are now desperately seeking 'something'. But without awareness, we do not know what we are looking for and it is very easy to miss the moment. Getting out of our heads can be a hit-and-miss affair, and without wisdom it makes no sense when we 'come back down to Earth'.

The search for spiritual meaning has taken us across space and out of time chasing angels and aliens, only to leave us feeling even more alienated. The quest for wholeness has taken us across the globe to remote hideaways in order to find ourselves, only to leave us just as lost when we return. In fact, we need look no further than beneath our very noses! **We need only come home to our bodies in order to embody Spirit** – we cannot be whole until we fully inhabit our physical vehicle, until we are wholly present in the body.

Heaven is not a place out there somewhere, but a state of being to be found right here, right now! Ecstasy is not an abnormal out-of-the-body experience reserved for mystics and madmen, nor is it just a weekend extravaganza. It is, in fact, a direct and tangible experience of Spirit available to each of us in every moment. Ecstasy is an awakening of the life force within us, the fusion between Spirit and Matter. Ecstasy is as natural as breathing, it is our birthright. And now is the perfect time for humanity to awaken to its ecstatic nature.

This book is a wake-up call! Now is the time to find freedom from the bondage of your own mind. This book is an invitation to get out of your head, come into your body and be filled with Spirit. You cannot save the world, but you can do something about your own little world. And what a difference this would make if we all did our little bit: **change yourself and you change the world!** The starting point to transformation is your*self* and your self lives in your body – not in your mind, as you'd like to believe.

This book will invite, ignite, inspire and instruct you to get out of your head and expand your vision of life, to become greater than who you think you are and experience the power of your being. When you awaken to your true nature, you will find that life is joyful, magical, ecstatic.

This book is an invitation to freedom. This book is an invitation from me … the Urban Mystic.

Teachings of an Urban Mystic

My teaching is simple: **get out of your head and into your body**. In other words, stop thinking and move! Movement is life!

For years, I was a big thinker. I swotted at school from the age of 4 and got grade A's when other kids were playing tag in the park. I read Jung and Solzenitzyn in my teens when other boys and girls were smoking cigarettes behind the bike shed. I spent twelve years studying psychology at university whilst other students were letting their hair down at parties. Throughout, I was depressed, lethargic and lifeless. I had studied psychology in order to understand the meaning of Existence, but there was no meaning to my life. I wanted to help my fellow man – and woman – but I could not help myself. Someone once said, I can't remember whom exactly: 'Studying the complexities of the mind may make you a good psychologist, but it won't take you beyond "mind".' Now I understand.

At the lowest point of my existential angst, I abandoned my academic vocation to go on an inner voyage of consciousness-exploration. My journey of self-discovery began in 1989 and, of course, still continues. The first seven years, however, were the most intense: I felt as if I had fallen down a crack that had suddenly appeared in my world, as if I had opened Pandora's box to unleash both Heaven and Hell. During this time, I travelled out of my body to meet cosmic beings in other dimensions that told me all about life and the universe. I travelled back in time to relive my childhood traumas, over and over again until the primal scream became just a distant whisper. I traversed both time and space to visit my past lives and balance out my karma. Several times I took a trip to India to meet holy men and contemplate my navel, amongst other things. And many more times, I tuned in, dropped one – or two – and tripped out … *far* out!

My search for wholeness has led me right back to where I am – **in my body**. The more I am fully present in my body, the more I am aware that movement is the integral nature of Existence. Just as night turns to day and winter turns to spring, everything changes. Just as clouds drift across the sky and water forever flows, life is in constant movement. The orbiting of the planets, the rotating of the Earth, the spinning of electrons – all these are part of the universal dance of life.

When my body moves, I move beyond my thoughts. I have discovered that the more I get myself, in other words, my 'thinker', out of the way, the more room there is for Spirit. The more I empty myself, the more I am filled with the divine … and life becomes ecstatic! The more I experience Spirit in my body, the more real I become, and the more at one I feel with myself and the world around me. I have seen behind the illusion of who I 'think' I am. I have seen beyond the dream of material reality. To me, everything is consciousness, everything is connected. To me, God/Goddess is everywhere and the purpose to my existence is union with All That Is. I am an urban mystic and my spirituality exists right here in the marketplace of today. Life exists only in the present and when we are also fully present, then life becomes a gift. Ecstasy is the experience of this gift. In other words, a state of deep joy and wonder at the magic and mystery of life.

Over the years, I have learnt to bridge the worlds of Spirit and Matter and so I am able to find joy amidst the mayhem of my urban world. I live in one of the biggest, busiest, most modern cities in the world. I live at a time when things are evolving very fast. I live with the crazy paradox of materialism and mysticism. Never before has there been such rampant worldwide consumerism sitting side-by-side with a growing global awareness of spirituality. I cannot hide and I cannot run away. There is nowhere to go but here. This is my reality. I am a product of this time in history. But I am also a mystic.

My journey has led me to create 'Moving into Ecstasy', a system of teachings which bring together ancient wisdom with modern techniques to heal mind, body and soul. 'Moving into Ecstasy' is a synthesis of many paths – knowing that they all lead to the One. My work weaves together

Movement Therapy, Breathwork, Bioenergetics, Chakra-work, Tantric Energy Techniques, Creative Visualization, Meditation, Trance-dance and Shamanism. I have borrowed, adapted and invented a whole host of processes to create a unique path relevant to today's world. In particular, my deep involvement with rebirthing has provided the groundwork for my emphasis on conscious connected breathing and my taste of Tantra has flavoured everything I teach. I am also greatly indebted to the enlightened rebel and unorthodox master, Osho, whose 'active meditations' never fail to move me into wholeness. Above and beyond all, I am forever grateful to Great Spirit/God/Goddess/All That Is/Whatever You Want to Call It for this Great Magical Mystery Tour Called Life!

My inspiration has and always will be finding new ways to embrace ourselves and extend ourselves out to the world. My name, Amoda, means 'joy' in Sanskrit and I am always seeking ways to bring that joy into day-to-day life. I am an urban mystic and my task is to wake you up, shake you up, show you a few tricks of the trade to help you become greater than who you think you are.

This book is my gift to you.

Chapter 2

Get Out of Your Head

> *'Are their heads off?' shouted the Queen.*
> *'Their heads are off, if it please your majesty!' the soldiers*
> *shouted in reply.*

LEWIS CARROLL, *Alice in Wonderland*

The Fall from Grace

Ever since Eve offered Adam the fruit of temptation, we have split ourselves in two. The story of Adam and Eve is one of separation, alienation and sin. It is the story of man vs. woman, humanity vs. Nature, and mind vs. body. Ever since humans became *self*-conscious, in other words, ashamed of their true nature, we have become divided against ourselves.

Most people, if asked where their mind is, will undoubtedly point to their head. If asked where their consciousness is, they will also point to their head. Somewhere long ago, our consciousness split off from our bodies and took up residence inside the bony structure above our necks. It is now a common and widespread belief that the mind is synonymous with the physical brain and that consciousness is a by-product of this highly complex bio-computer.

This belief has a profound effect on how we view the world. If we believe that information about the world enters only through the holes in our head, then our perception of reality is limited to this experience. If we do not see with our whole being, then we do not see the whole world. If we limit consciousness, mind and intelligence to the mass of biological wiring inside our skulls, then we cut ourselves off at the neck. Anything below this point is unconscious, mindless, unintelligent. This separation is at the root of our suffering. Separation from the totality of our nature has created guilt. We are ashamed of who we really are, of our less conscious parts, our bodies. This is the true meaning of sin.

This is the 'fall from grace'. It is not that God has punished us for tasting the delights of the flesh: **the fall from grace is simply the loss of wholeness**. We have become fragmented, alienated from ourselves and from the Source of Life. We have lost our ecstatic nature, for ecstasy cannot happen without wholeness. This loss of wholeness is the source of our pain. Deep down in our souls we yearn for the experience of ecstasy, for the return to blissful Oneness.

It is not that God has banished us from Eden ... rather it is us who have banished Him, or maybe I should say Her.

God versus Goddess

The expulsion from Paradise started in pre-*hist*ory. It was a time of *her*-story, a time when God and Goddess were united. Men and women lived peacefully, in harmony with each other and with their planetary home. They honoured their own bodies as they honoured the body of the Earth. Everything was alive and everything was connected. Earth was Gaia, the Great Goddess, the Mother of Creation. And just as Spirit was manifest in Matter, so *God* was contained within *Goddess*. The body was the temple of Spirit and ecstasy was a direct religious experience. The celebration of sexuality, dance and ritual was an expression of divine Oneness.

For millennia, these matriarchal tribes lived in a state of wholeness, in touch with their own natural cycles and the cycles of Nature. The nature of their consciousness was holistic, and through it they were able to perceive the totality of Existence and the interconnected nature of all things. To them, the 'seen' and 'unseen' realities overlapped and consciousness could move freely between the worlds of Matter and Spirit.

However, the essence of Existence is a natural yin-yang polarity, which swings from feminine to masculine and back again in huge cycles of time. At the turn of one of these cycles, about 5,000 years ago, things started to change. Marauding tribes from Eurasia descended on the gentle hunter-gatherers who lovingly roamed the Earth and imposed their patriarchal ways. These invading peoples saw the forces of Nature as something to fight against, something to be tamed and controlled. Just as Spirit was driven out of body, so God became divorced from Goddess – and so started the war on ecstasy.

As the masculine principles of logic, morality and organization took over, art, ritual and magic were pushed aside. In their place grew agriculture, architecture and industry. The domestication of animals for food and for labour and the development of permanent dwellings to keep out the forces of Nature severed the link with the spirit of the Earth. As the accumulation of wealth became a sign of strength, natural resources became a commodity. As trade and commerce became the cornerstones of daily life, control and competitiveness became necessary survival skills – and so civilization was born.

As the feminine principles of intuition, sensuality and chaos were suppressed, all that was natural became feared. The body became shameful, sex became sinful and ecstasy was denied. Eve, became Evil, the temptress who led men astray, the Devil who delighted in the flesh and invited the wrath of God – guilt is indeed a terrible punishment! And what became of Adam? Well, he got everything 'back to front' and so became mad. (Adam spelt backwards is 'mad(a)'! Do I really need to spell it out for you?) In other words, he lost himself and his sense of reality; he lost touch with Nature and with his naturalness. And so *her*-story became *his*-story. And apparently – so we are told – that was the beginning of mankind. Alas it was also the end of womankind.

The final blow for matriarchy came from organized religion. (How can true religion, that highly personal experience of God, ever be organized?!) The spread of Judeo-Christianity was the death of the wild, chaotic, ecstatic feminine. It was also the death of millions of women – and a fair few men – branded as witches, whores and heretics and eternally damned to Hell. The legacy of this has lasted long: even today, sex, ecstasy and magic are eyed with suspicion.

As God took over from Goddess, a **dominator** model of society replaced the old **partnership** style. Goddess knows that male and female are inseparable, forever dancing together in ecstatic partnership, just as the nature of Existence is both yin and yang. But God decided to exercise his authority and dropped her to become 'God the Almighty'. He is the god of law and order, issuing commands and meting out punishment. 'Our Father' now sits 'up there', in Heaven, whilst we mere mortals suffer down here. Heaven is an imaginary, perfect place, far away from the messy affairs of humans. Spirit has been torn from flesh and what is 'down there' is dark and dirty. And what is in the dark is unseen and so remains unconscious.

Consciousness has been elevated – in other words, made higher, more dignified, more worthy – to the space between our ears. It's a small space so it must be a small consciousness! Squeezed into this bony box, we are top-heavy and about to topple over. We are out of balance – and so is the Earth. We have created a world full of violence and war because we are violent towards our own bodies and at war with our true nature. The cruel violation of those 'weaker' than ourselves, such as children, animals and minority races, is a mirror of the denial of our own vulnerability. The rape and abuse of women is synonymous with the rape and abuse of our planet. In the separation of mind and body, we have alienated our souls. This heartless destruction of anything that happens to be around is surely destroying us.

We have allowed our heads to rule our hearts and this is an unhealthy situation. We have limited our understanding of the world to the information that comes through the small apertures in our heads – the eyes, nose and ears. These sensory organs analyse, discriminate and organize our perception of reality. In return, we spew out of another aperture in our heads – the mouth – a linear and sequential translation of this information, logically arranged as a series of sounds called language. (Now that was quite a mouthful!) Surely this cannot be the whole picture?

Thinking has become our primary mode of being. We are proud to say that thinking is a human trait that differentiates us from every other living creature! 'I think, therefore I am' is a philosophical, but erroneous, statement that has become imprinted in our historical memory. Perhaps it would be better to say 'I am, therefore I think … and feel, love, hate, eat, sleep, etc.'! It is not that thinking is wrong in itself, for without that logical, rational part of us we, and our world, would be a chaotic mess! The thinking part of the mind acts as a safety valve, filtering out the avalanche of images, sensations, impressions and feelings that would otherwise overwhelm us. So it is not that we should stop thinking. As Eckhart Tolle (spiritual teacher and author of *The Power of Now*) says, it is simply that 'thinking has become a disease … and disease is what happens when we are out of balance'.

Small-mindedness

Today, we live in a world far-removed from a natural state of harmony – we are indeed out of balance. We have lost our centre and forgotten that life's journey is a spiral path. Instead, we have taken off on a linear trajectory of ever-increasing industrialization and urbanization. The end result has been a wake of destruction, yet we pride ourselves in calling this 'civilization'. Such a blinkered outlook has been mirrored by the myopic mechanistic paradigm of science. In this view, the universe is nothing more than a giant machine, a series of separate and ordered building blocks, which we can chop and change according to our whims. Science zooms in on the detail, dissecting information in a reductionist-style analysis, forgetting that **the whole is greater than the sum of the parts**. Science believes that the mind lives in the brain, losing sight of the greater truth and missing out on the intricate beauty and mystery of life.

This lopsided view of reality is exactly that ... lopsided! Rather than branding the mind as 'wrong', it is more accurate to say that the *thinking* mind is a function of one side of the brain and therefore unbalanced. Just as the nature of Existence is yin-yang, so our physical nature reflects this male-female polarity. It makes sense, then, that the brain, which is simply the receiver for all the information that exists, also mirrors this duality.

The brain has two hemispheres, the left and the right. The left deals with ordinary day-to-day consciousness. It is logical, analytical, linear, sequential and causal. It is the part of you that successfully masters the latest computer software and that carefully plans your weekly schedule. It is also the part of you that drives a car without forgetting to put the brakes on at the red lights and that knows not to stick your hand in the fire just because it looks so welcoming. Abstract concepts, rules and regulations, perfection and performance – these are all qualities of the masculine principle at work in the left brain hemisphere. This is the world of the archetypal male – the go-getting, forward-thrusting, high-flying, incisive, decisive superhero. This is the domain of God.

The right side of the brain deals with non-ordinary states of consciousness. It is non-rational, non-verbal, non-spatial, intuitive, timeless and simultaneous. Here, the normal boundaries of perception are transcended. This is the world of dreams, symbolism and art. It is the part of you that is moved by a piece of music, that hears poetry in the song of a bird, that sees lifetimes of experience in a newborn's eyes. It is also the part of you that wants to 'go out to play', that loves to dress up and have fun on the dance floor. Empathy, sensitivity, playfulness, spontaneity and wildness – these are qualities of the feminine principle. This is the world of the archetypal female – the gentle, sensual, seductive, curvaceous, changeable, crazy, chaotic Maiden-Mother-Crone. This is the domain of Goddess.

The modern urban world is decidedly one-sided, greatly favouring the left/masculine over the right/feminine. The religious and cultural heritage of the Judeo-Christian system has left us with a monotheistic, authoritarian outlook that is deeply ingrained in our thinking. In other words, there is only one God and He is an angry old man who tells us what is right and what is wrong. You don't have to believe in God in order to have swallowed this lie. If you look honestly, you will see that you constantly judge yourself and others. The educational and cultural legacy of 2,000 years of dogma and indoctrination has left us with a hierarchical system where 'survival of the fittest' is something to be encouraged above and beyond everything else. Striving to get to the top of the achievement ladder is deemed a worthwhile endeavour: competition, not co-operation, is seen as a sign of strength.

For many years, I believed that I was not good enough unless I reached the highest pinnacle of academic success. I had to be better than everyone else, better than the best, the absolute top in my highly specialized field. For years, I believed that I would be punished, in other words, banished/not loved, if I did not get this external approval from the world. I was searching for my father's love, but what I was really doing was begging God to accept me.

Whether we like it or not, we have inherited a system of beliefs from our history, our society and our family. We are conditioned, programmed to think this is who we are. But this is a false self because it is not the whole story. We are disempowered because we are not complete; we are just a small part of our whole selves. How can we be truly powerful if we are small? Dig deep enough and we all have some of these limiting beliefs.

● ●

Here are some common limiting beliefs that we are programmed to believe. Try them out and see if you have a strong reaction to any of them. The stronger your reaction, the more likely that this belief system is deeply embedded in your unconscious and is keeping you 'small'.

'I have to work hard to survive.'
'There's not enough money to go round in the world.'
'Money is the root of all evil.'
'Money doesn't grow on trees.'
'Life is a bitch and then you die!'
'I'm too old to do that.'
'I'm too old to fall in love.'
'Love never lasts.'
'Nobody loves me.'
'I'm not good enough.'
'I can't do that.'
'There's never enough time.'
'I might fail and then where would I be?'
'It's not spiritual to act like that.'

19

'God/life/whatever will punish me if I do that.'
'I don't deserve it.'
'Nothing ever works out for me.'
'My family screwed me up – it's not my fault.'
'I've had a hard life – what do you expect?'
'It just isn't the done thing!'
'What will the neighbours think?'
… and so on and so on!

● ●

This is just the voice of the **small mind**, the mind that thinks it knows, when, in fact, it has no wisdom. This is the part that lives in the past and in the future, the part that remembers old wounds, worries about consequences, plans for a rainy day and hopes for a brighter future. This part lives in the illusory world of time, out of touch with reality and out of touch with the true nature of self. This is the **small self**, waiting to break free.

● ●

Try this – an experiment in **looking**. Try not to **think** about it, just **look** at the hard facts! It's very simple really!

Look ... No Head!

• Point to something – anything, an object in the room you are in.
  What do you see, what are you pointing at?
  (Answer: a book, a TV screen, a flower, a mug, etc.)

- Now turn your finger round and point to yourself, to the place where your face is. What are you pointing at?
  (Answer: **no-thing** ... no face, no head, just emptiness!)

- Now just look down at yourself from your standing position. What do you see?
  (Answer: shoulders, chest, arms, torso, legs, feet ... but **no head**!)

- What do you actually see in place of your head?
  (Answer: **every-thing** ... the whole world around me!)

(ADAPTED FROM DOUGLAS HARDING, *The Headless Way*)

● ●

Chapter 3

Free Your Mind

Losing your mind can be a peak experience.

Jane Wagner

Voices in Your Head

Small may be beautiful when it comes to the latest telecommunications technology, the monthly bills, or the size of your bottom ... but when we're talking about the mind, then big is definitely better! **Small mind is limitation, big mind is freedom**.

Small mind is what most of us use most of the time. It is the part of us that tells us 'do this' or 'don't do that'. It is the part that criticizes, compares, justifies and makes excuses. It is the part that is ready to attack, defend and hide. Small mind is self-centred, in other words, concerned with its own survival. It keeps us separate ... I am 'in here' and the Big Bad World is 'out there'. **Small mind is the ego**, the part that acts like an executive, making decisions and making sure they are carried out. And like any self-respecting businessperson, the ego's primary goals are self-profit and self-protection. This is the **personal will**.

Small mind is also the **personality**, the part that I think is uniquely me. If you were asked who you are, you would probably give your name and occupation, and then you might say, 'I am so-and-so's wife/husband/sister/ mother/father, I am a loving friend, a good cook, a careful driver.' If asked to describe yourself further, you might say, 'I am spiritual, creative, hard-working, clever, caring, honest, good-natured.' These are the things that define you in relation to your world. Mostly, these are also things that you have been conditioned to believe about yourself and your world. If you look carefully, you can see that there are a number of 'yous', each one ready to take centre stage depending on the circumstances. If you look even closer, you can also see that there are a number of yous that have been pushed away, that take a back seat. If you allow these hidden yous to have a voice, you can also say 'I am bossy, I am shy, I am serious, silly, scared, sexy, lazy, jealous, angry, crazy' … I could go on. These are your sub-personalities, the many voices in your head that each have something to say.

● ●

Here are some voices or sub-personalities that we all have in common. See which ones you can identify in yourself.

THE SLAVE-DRIVER:

'I have to finish this project on time!'

'I have to get all the washing up done before so and so gets home!'

'I have to fix that leaky tap!'

'I must do 300 sit-ups today!'

'There's not enough time to do everything I need to.'

… and so on!

THE SUPER-CRITIC:

'I didn't do that as well as I could have done.'

'I'm not thin enough yet.'

'I'm not attractive enough.'

'My hair's not quite right.'

'My stomach's not flat enough.'

'My house/car/wallet isn't big enough.'

… and so on!

THE ABSOLUTE PERFECTIONIST:

'I must tidy everything up.'

'I mustn't make any mistakes.'

'I must look good/be polite/smell nice/etc. all the time.'

'Those flowers absolutely have to match the colour of the sofa!'

… and so on!

THE POWER ADDICT:

'I must be a millionaire by the time I'm 30!'

'I must become director of the company.'

'I must write a bestseller!'

'I must have a no.1 hit in the charts!'

… and so on!

THE SORRY PLEASER:

'I must make sure the kids are always happy.'

'I must be a good partner at all costs.'

'I mustn't make so-and-so angry or else I'll be sorry.'

'I must do/say the right thing so that so-and-so will like me.'

… and so on!

THE POOR-ME VICTIM:

'Things always go wrong for me.'

'No one understands me.'

'It's all my fault.'

'Life is so hard.'

'I can't do that – I'm too poor/too ugly/too underqualified/too scared.'

… and so on!

And here are some commonly disowned voices:

THE FRAGILE CHILD:

'I'm frightened of revealing who I really am – maybe no one will like me.'

'I'm afraid no one will really listen.'

'I'm afraid of being hurt again.'

… and so on!

THE MAGICAL PLAYFUL CHILD:

'I can do whatever I want, whenever I want.'

'It's fun to be silly.'

'Isn't life wonderful? It's full of magic and mystery.'

'I'm going to wish on a rainbow!'

… and so on!

THE SEX-POT:

'I love my body and I love others to love it too.'

'I am a powerful sexual being … and it's great!'

'Sex is an act of beauty.'

'I honour the God/Goddess in me.'

'I just love men/women/both!'

... and so on!

THE DEVIL INCARNATE:

'I'm pissed off with you/the world/everything!'

'I want to destroy everything in my path ... so get out of my way!'

'I'm really not very nice, so beware!'

'I could kill you!'

'I want everything for myself!'

'I'll do anything to get what I want!'

... and so on!

● ●

Small mind is like a monkey: it likes to chatter. Small or 'monkey' mind is always there, sniffing out potential threats, looking out for tit-bits to feed its paranoia, and jumping to conclusions. To small mind, life is an endless series of problems to be assessed and solved. It is afraid of the unknown and so is always on guard. It likes things to be tidy, organized and safe. But this sense of security, this belief of being in charge, in control, is actually an illusion. Small mind actually has no free will, even though it totally believes it has. At this stage of development, the ego is fully identified with the sub-personalities, the voices, and so has lost its true executive function as 'choice-maker'. Small mind is like being asleep: at this level, you are unconscious.

The ego has been given bad press in the self-help community: there is talk of 'killing' the ego in order to advance spiritually. But it cannot be annihilated because it is a part of us, albeit a small part. As Ekhart Tolle says: 'The mind is not dysfunctional. It is a wonderful tool. Dysfunction sets in when you seek yourself in it and mistake it for who you are.' In other words, it is the ego's identification with the sub-personalities that is dysfunctional. In fact, the stronger the identification, the higher the neurosis level! The more wrapped up we are in our many selves, the more trapped we are in our conditioning.

The way out of this bondage is the ego's *disidentification* with the sub-personalities. Separation, not death, is the answer – although it may feel like death to the ego! We cannot get rid of small mind, hard as we try, and trying makes it harder, but we can get to see beyond it. By just watching the many selves play out their roles, by just hearing the many voices clamouring for attention, we can start to disengage. By not giving this endless stream of thoughts much attention, by just bearing witness without giving it much energy, we can start to realize the illusory nature of small mind. This is the seed of awareness – and **awareness is the key to freedom**.

By stepping back from the petty chatter of small mind, we expand our awareness and we step into big mind. As the ego separates from the many selves, it moves into higher levels of consciousness and becomes an aware ego. Now it is able to make choices based on a higher viewpoint. Now you are awake, now you can make a conscious choice! It is as if you have some breathing room now. There is time to choose your response rather than just react blindly. This is **free will**.

So, rather than seeing small or 'monkey' mind as something totally worthless, we can see it as an awakener of awareness. It is precisely by becoming aware of the nature of small mind that our awareness grows into big mind. There is an old Zen saying: 'You should be grateful for the weeds you have in your mind because eventually they will enrich you.' In the Eastern traditions of Buddhism, Hinduism and Taoism, the monkey is seen as a helpful albeit mischievous guide. Here, Monkey is a trickster, a fool in disguise, who, by his very antics, tricks us into seeing a greater picture of the world.

And so it is with small mind. By bringing our attention to the ego-games we play, by embracing our many voices rather than pushing them away, we actually expand our consciousness. Without this stimulus, this impetus to rise above them, we would not grow. It is one of those great paradoxes that life likes to present us with!

Climb to the Peak

Big mind is expanded consciousness. It is consciousness freed from its habitual prison-like home, the head. Once freed, it is no longer bound by the limitations of the small self. It is no longer separate from the greater whole, therefore fear is no longer its guiding strategy. Without separation, there is no need for protection or profit. If you are a part of everything else, then you have no need for defence or attack or gain. Big mind is all-inclusive: it is the realization that consciousness is everywhere and everything is inter-connected.

This view is supported by the findings of both physicists and consciousness-researchers at the leading edge of the 'new science'. In essence, this 'holographic model' sees both the universe and consciousness as a whole system, a hologram, where every part can reconstruct the whole. This is the true nature of reality. You and Existence are actually one. There is no separation, no duality, no fight, no struggle. This is surrender to What Is – the present moment. This is the experience of getting out of your head, when time stands still and thoughts disappear. Reality can only exist in the present moment, the Now. Everything else is an illusion, a fantasy. Small mind lives in the past and future. The past is gone and the future is yet to come, so how can these exist? **Only NOW is real!**

This *realization* is freedom. It is like being a bird soaring high above, able to see clearly. Once consciousness is freed from its bondage, the true nature of self is revealed. It is not that small mind is destroyed, but rather that it is transcended. Big mind contains small mind within it (remember, big mind is all-inclusive!). As consciousness expands, it moves beyond the realm of the personal and into the transpersonal. This is 'sky mind' or 'universal mind'. It is the place of intuition, inspiration and illumination. It is from this expanded viewpoint that great insights are made, creative genius is born and mystical revelation is granted.

From this place, you can see into a previously unsolvable problem because you look from a higher perspective. It is from here that great scientists like Francis Crick envisioned the double-helix structure of DNA, and that creative geniuses like Albert Einstein came up with the Theory of Relativity. It is from here that great mystics like William Blake can perceive 'a world in a grain of sand and heaven in a flower' and visionary authors like Aldous Huxley can construct 'a brave new world'. From this place, you are filled with wonder and awe because a mystery of Nature is revealed. It is from here that great mystics like Rumi proclaim that 'we are as mountains and the echo within is from thee' and Kahlil Gibran speaks of '(the) blood (that is) the sap that feeds the tree of heaven'.

It is from this exalted standpoint that Nirvana/the Light/the Source/God is experienced. This is Christ-consciousness, Buddha-Nature, the Centre: this is enlightenment. It is not that the many selves do not exist any more, rather that when you stand in your centre, you can see who you really are and so you do not identify with these voices. Enlightenment is not obliteration of the personality, but a transcendence of it: in other words, it is being able to see beyond it. And like a bird, the higher you fly, the clearer you can see. The more consciousness expands, the more you are at one with All That Is and the closer you are to the realization that the ultimate nature of everything is nothing. Everything arises from nothing and ultimately goes back to nothing. This is the experience of the Void, no-mind, no-self. This is where the small self disappears and you are one with God. Now you are aligned to **divine will**.

Such dizzy heights are not just for the enlightened few. You do not have to climb a mountain and starve yourself in a dark cave for aeons in order to free your mind. Many mere mortals, like you and I, can have a **peak experience**. A peak experience is exactly what it says: an experience of a high, or expanded, state of consciousness. Contrary to spiritual scriptures, it does not require an eternity of ascetic practice and initiation into some secret sect. It can happen to anyone at any time – it is, after all, natural. What is more natural than an orgasm, and what is an orgasm if not a peak experience?

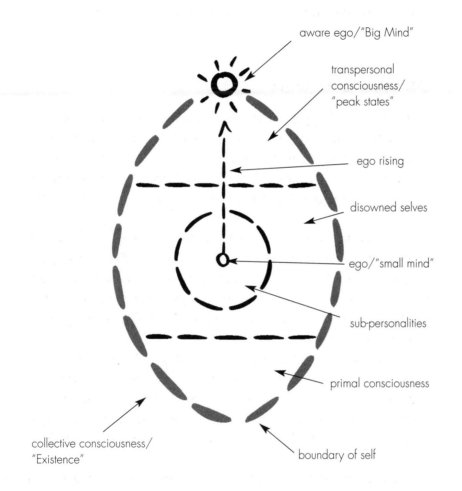

aware ego/"Big Mind"

transpersonal
consciousness/
"peak states"

ego rising

disowned selves

ego/"small mind"

sub-personalities

primal consciousness

collective consciousness/
"Existence"

boundary of self

EGO RISING

A peak experience is a state of ecstasy. As you lose your 'self' in the moment, you merge with the One. This merging is the experience of joy, bliss, ecstasy.

Spiritual Emergence

It is thanks to the great grandfather of transpersonal psychology, Abraham Maslow, that investigations into 'how humans tick' have turned away from the study of the dysfunctional psyche towards the study of the healthy psyche. Prior to the 1950s, it appeared that we were all miserable, neurotic half-wits! Since then, it has been acknowledged that happiness is normal and healthy!

Maslow found that a certain section of society, classified as 'high achievers', experienced moments of such intense joy and happiness that the nitty-gritty struggle and hum-drum repetition of daily routine faded away, that a jaded outlook became repainted in vibrancy and depth, and that life was bursting with flavourful possibilities. It is Maslow who called these moments 'peak experiences'. He also found that these 'peakers' were more creative, more successful, more fulfilled and more psychologically healthy than the vast majority of the population. These were people who had tasted ecstasy, even for a moment. And once tasted, never forgotten … Such a glimpse of freedom is often more than enough to make a difference to the way daily life is perceived. Life becomes more meaningful, more joyful, more worthwhile.

But Maslow never went on to study why or how these wonderful experiences occurred. Since his seminal research, studies have shown that there are certain triggers likely to induce peak experiences. Most often, an overwhelming emotion is the catalyst. It could be something of extraordinary beauty that simply 'takes your breath away': natural wonders such as gigantic mountain ranges, enormous waterfalls, vast deserts or magical sunsets. Or it could be the death of a loved one, a broken love affair, a financial disaster, the loss of a job. Accidents, operations, serious illness, sleep deprivation, prolonged physical exertion, childbirth and even passionate lovemaking are well reported triggers. When such a situation activates a sudden intense feeling, we may be shocked out of our usual way of seeing things. In particular, there are many cases cited of near-death experiences where a momentary glimpse of something 'other' is enough to completely transform someone's attitude to life. One example is that of Foster Perry who was struck by lightning and then went on to become a renowned healer with the ability to see deeply into the spiritual dimension of other people's lives. There are extensive case studies of people who have 'died' and come back with a renewed sense of joy in life.

Dr Stanislav Grof, who is responsible for a vast bulk of this research over the past twenty-five years or so, calls these events 'spiritual emergencies'. He has found that such experiences lead to improved psychological and physical health, a sense of personal freedom and empowerment, a deeper connection with other people, Nature and the universe, and an awareness of the spiritual dimension of life.

Today, it seems that these spiritual emergencies are more common. More and more people, from a wider range of backgrounds, are experiencing glimpses of freedom, whether it be just for a moment or something more enduring. It seems that as society moves out of the 'dominator' pattern, we are more likely to experience holistic states of mind.

Perhaps a crucial factor has been the resurgence of interest in spiritual practices, and particularly those that include some element of physical involvement. Tantric energy-work, breath therapy, Kundalini yoga, trance-dancing, Shamanic drumming and chanting are just some of the techniques that have been traditionally used for transcendence and are now enjoying a revival.

Whatever the situation, whatever the method, it is clear that during these peak experiences the thinking mind is no longer in charge, no longer the boss. In these moments, all duality is transcended and a holistic framework exists. This unified consciousness is an indicator of left and right brain synchronization, hence the reported increases in creativity, intuition, extra-sensory perception and relaxation following a peak experience. It is the same state of consciousness that is achieved by meditation practice.

Many years ago, before I even knew of the word 'meditation', I had my first peak experience. In the midst of my depressive phase, I had discovered that the only thing that would jolt me out of the blues was to run – and to keep on running. Over a year or so, I worked my way up from huffing round the block for 10 minutes to training for the London Marathon with twenty-mile runs! It was somewhere around the seven-mile mark that something started to shift. My perception was heightened as the leaves on the trees became a dazzling kaleidoscope of colours and the sound of the birds became a divine song. My worries faded into the background as I was filled with a sense of awe at the miracle of life and my heart burst open. My body glided with ease as I surged forward through a web of interconnecting streams of energy and I became one with the world. I was flying – flying high as my spirit soared.

Since then, I have experienced many more peaks, each one just as beautiful as the one before. Over time, I have integrated these experiences so that they form an underlying thread of meaning in my life. I have transformed a 'spiritual emergency' into a 'spiritual emergence'. However, such a transformation is not always easy. Without guidance and grounding, it is easy to get lost. Without awareness and integration, it is easy to suffer the pitfalls.

The increase of experimentation with mind-altering substances for recreation is especially dangerous. Apart from the physiological side effects of consistent chemical intoxication, once the 'doors of perception' are opened who knows what will be encountered. The difference between someone who has prepared for the dissolution of 'self' boundaries and someone who hasn't is akin to the difference between jumping out of a plane with a parachute and falling out accidentally.

A few years ago, when I was writing for magazines on the topic of spiritual emergence within dance culture, I received hundreds of letters from young people who desperately wanted guidance. Many of them had inadvertently awakened to their spiritual nature through the use of psychoactives, but most of them felt as if they were losing their mind. Without pointers along the way, they were getting lost, feeling alone and ungrounded.

Getting high is not something to be messed around with: it requires preparation and awareness – these are the cornerstones of my teaching.

Chapter 4

Prepare for God ... and Wait!

There is no time, no place, no state where God is absent.

MARIANNE WILLIAMSON

Sweet Surrender

Getting high is not something you can 'get'. It is not something you can achieve, accomplish, attain or acquire. Nor is it something you can grasp, hold on to or possess. It is not an object, a product or a commodity. Such a goal-orientated attitude is small-minded and therefore self-centred. Separation, competition and gratification are exactly the qualities that prevent the experience of freedom.

It is a beautiful paradox that in seeking freedom we are required to let go of the seeker. The truth is always a paradox, just as the whole is always made up of opposites – yin and yang/male and female/dark and light etc. To be free requires surrender, letting go, a state of being not doing. And yet we must also desire freedom, we must move towards it, make an effort. Surrender is not weakness, not laziness, not sleepiness: it does not come from the place of the victim. On the contrary, surrender is complete wakefulness, being totally and utterly here and now: this is the place of empowerment. You could call this state 'alert passivity'. The Taoists call it 'actionless activity', the Zen Buddhists call it 'no-mind', others have called it 'witnessing' and 'headlessness'. This is the state known as *wu wei*, the 'soft strength' or 'hidden power', that is cultivated in martial arts such as t'ai chi, wu shu and kung fu. In the ancient Tantric teachings of the Indian master Tilopa, there is a song which encapsulates this attitude:

> *'Be like a hollow bamboo ... do nought with your body but relax; shut firm the mouth and silent remain ... and suddenly infinite energy starts pouring within you. Become like a hollow bamboo, nothing inside. And suddenly the moment you are a hollow bamboo, the divine lips are on you, the hollow bamboo becomes a flute, and the song starts.'*

I like to say: **'Spirit fills you when you are empty.'** In other words, first get your 'self' out of the way and then be like an empty vessel, waiting to be filled. The doing, the work, the effort is in the preparation. The preparation involves making yourself empty, getting your small self out of the way – and this requires some work. Once you have done all the preparation you can, then you can just let go, give up all the effort, surrender – there is nothing more you can do. Now you are like a cup waiting to be filled by the grace of God/Goddess/Universal Intelligence/Spirit; it happens when you are ready. If you are not ready, if you are unprepared, you will miss the moment. You will be so trapped in your many selves that there will be no room for Spirit. Another way of saying it is: **'Prepare for God ... and wait!'**

● ●

This is an adaptation of a Tantric energy exercise, traditionally called *Latihan*: it is incredibly powerful and healing when the full process is completed, but even a taste will do!

Make sure you are alone and will not be disturbed, that you are in silence and that there is no rush. Take as much time as you need; the longer you can do this for, the more powerful the experience. However, this may be quite difficult to do at first because the Western mind finds it hard to do nothing. Keep trying anyway – even a few minutes is good.

Be Like a Hollow Bamboo

Stand with your feet firm but the rest of the body as relaxed and loose as possible; close your eyes.

Do absolutely nothing! Just have an attitude of waiting, as if a special guest is about to arrive. The most important thing is to keep your body as loose as possible: knees soft, muscles around the genitals and anus relaxed, belly and buttocks relaxed, spine yielding, shoulders, arms, hands very loose, neck and face relaxed. Imagine you are like a piece of bamboo just standing there, rooted to the ground but yielding to the wind when it comes.

After a while, you will find that the body starts to make small movements on its own, as if it is swaying or bending or turning – allow these to happen naturally, do not control the movements but just co-operate with them. Eventually, you will find that some of these movements may become stronger and wilder. Imagine there is nothing inside you; you are like a hollow bamboo, just empty. With time, you will get a sense of being filled with something, a subtle energy that may cause the body to vibrate or tingle – just enjoy it! You may even feel as if you have been filled with a divine presence.

● ●

Personally, I have learnt this over and over again. I have a burning desire for both the spiritual search and for creative self-expression. The spiritual and creative paths actually follow the same map. Imagine the creative 'birth-process' you would go through in writing a poem or a piece of music. In setting out your vision for the creation, you are striving for your highest creative expression. There are two ways of doing this. The first way is to use your logical mind, your small mind, to adhere to a strict timetable, an ordered sequence, a set of ideas that make sense. But this way, you are likely to get caught up in a vicious cycle of achievement and goals. In trying to think too hard of what you are going to do, you have strangled the flow, the creative life force has withered.

The second way is to step back a little and create some space, some emptiness. Usually this means taking time out to be silent, to meditate, to go for a long walk, to just be in Nature. Rather than filling your head up with what you should be doing, you are simply making some room for emptiness, simply clearing the clutter of your mind. In this way, you include your non-rational mind, your 'big mind', and so you start to see the bigger picture. You drop your thinking and **feel** your vision, and so the creation almost creates itself. It is like standing at the edge of the known and the unknown: it is here that true creativity – and true spirituality – is born.

This is the place of growth, of expansion, the edge from where you can leap and grow wings. This edge is usually experienced as some kind of resistance, a stuckness, a block. This is created by the thinking mind, the small self: if you stay at this edge and wait and do not try to think your way through, if you do not try to solve it, then the block will simply dissolve. You have to stand at the edge and wait for the resistance to dissolve, you have to let go of whom you think you are or what you think you are creating – you simply have to surrender. Buddhists calls this 'dying to the present moment'. This is the truly spiritual path and it is the truly creative path. It is true whether you are dealing with a difficult emotion, meditating, writing, painting or giving birth. And this is actually the crux of my teaching: taking you to the edge, finding ways of letting go, preparing you for the leap into the unknown.

Preparation, by definition, involves some kind of routine, a practice or discipline. Whichever path you choose to embark on, there is always a set of guidelines, a structure of some sort. And there are many paths to choose from! If you choose yoga as your path, there is Hatha, Ashtanga, Iyengar, Kundalini, and many others; if you choose Paganism, there is Druidry, Wicca, Goddess Worship, Nature Spirituality, and many others; if you choose Shamanism, there is Native American, Toltec, Mayan, Celtic, Neo-Shamanism; and so on and so on ad infinitum! In each of these, there is always some kind of teaching, a philosophy, a system of beliefs. This is knowledge and it is good and necessary on the path of self-development, in other words, when getting to know yourself. This practice, this discipline, this knowledge paves the way. It is preparation. But this is all it is – just preparation. Ultimately, all knowledge is useless!

Knowledge is the 'known' and what is known eventually becomes a limitation. Knowledge is accumulated by the thinking mind. We can go on and on gaining more and more knowledge about spiritual this and spiritual that, but spiritual consumerism does not make us spiritual! Knowing how many breaths to take in order to activate your Kundalini or how to prepare a sacred spell in order to attract the power of the Goddess is not the same as the actual experience of Spirit. Somewhere along the line, knowledge must be dropped. It is this surrender of what you think you know that allows you to open up to the unknown; it is only when the form is dropped that you can experience the formless. Surrender to the unknown — this is where the magic happens!

Surrendering to Spirit is a mystical experience. Mysticism is not the same as religion. Religion is the outer form of expression of the mystical experience. Religion is doing not being. This gives rise to beliefs, concepts, ideologies, dogmas. The path of the mystic is the path of devotion — it is of the heart not the intellect. If we come from the heart, then we transcend the mind and experience the bigger reality. This is a tough one for us 'civilized' Westerners, for we like to know, to understand, to hold onto some idea and put it into a known framework. But unfortunately, this is exactly the attitude that keeps us in our heads, in a limited reality, shut off from Existence.

Ultimately, all spiritual paths lead to the One. In other words, all spiritual practices are simply a preparation for the experience of Unity/God/Goddess/All That Is. In my search for Spirit, I have learnt this over and over again. Over the years, I have rebalanced my chakras with crystals placed in precise geometric order, I have chanted with Tibetan masters who initiated me into immortality, I have received secret teachings to re-activate my DNA,

41

and I have met the Cosmic Mother who impregnated me with the Golden Nectar of Life. Over the years, I have danced in and out of Buddhism, Shamanism and all manner of New Age-isms. Ultimately, I have discovered that enlightenment is not what I do, but what I am. Over the years, I have immersed myself in myriad forms of meditations, from Vippasana to Zazen, from Rigpa to Dzogchen, from TM to visualization, from concentration to contemplation. Ultimately, I have learnt that meditation is not something you do, but a state of being you experience when you stop doing.

• •

Here is something I wrote whilst in an expanded state of consciousness which, for me, encapsulated the nature of 'knowledge':

Knowledge is like a series of isolated islands of Illumination in a vast sea of Ignorance. Each one is an entity in its own right, different and apart from all the others, however close or far. But if we delve deeper into the pool of Unknown, we discover that these islands are actually just the peaks of vast mountains of Eternal Knowledge, like tips of icebergs barely visible above the icy water. And that these mountains all meet and join at the bottom, so that they blend into a common valley of Ultimate Truth. Only when we teach ourselves to take the plunge past our own boundaries and dive deep into ourselves can we finally discover that All Knowledge is One.

• •

The creation of 'Moving into Ecstasy' is a culmination of this understanding. I have drawn on many different sources, both ancient and modern, to find techniques that will move you from doing to being, that will help you jump from small mind to big mind, that will push you to the edge of the unknown. I have blended and adapted, borrowed and invented, a whole array of activities from the diversity of spiritual traditions around the world. I have woven the variety of strands into a cohesive whole that will get you 'out of your head' so that you can be who you really are.

My teachings are pathless; they simply point the way to Spirit. My teaching is the preparation; the rest is by the grace of God.

Heaven on Earth

Heaven and Earth have been divided for too long. Heaven is a place far, far away, a place we may or may not visit, depending on whether we have been 'good enough' in this lifetime. Certainly it is a place we visit only after our death, certainly without a body and certainly without anything material. This renunciation of all that is material is generally a feature of the spiritual life. Jesus sacrificed his body on the cross, Buddha renounced his princely empire to sit under the Bodhi tree, and the Virgin Mary gave birth to the Son of God without even having sex! Today, the holy men of India still wander the streets naked and penniless, Buddhist disciples abstain from worldly affairs in the search for reality, and millions of Christian monks and nuns deny themselves the pleasure of human touch. For too long, the spiritual path has been restrictive, repressive, ascetic and anti-life.

The recent revival of spirituality in the Western world has done little to bring Heaven any closer. The so-called 'New Age' has sometimes proved to be more 'the same old story'. Most extreme are the suicide cults of recent times, which have replayed the Biblical belief that Heaven is only for the dead. One of the most publicized is that of the Heaven's Gate community, in which hundreds of people were persuaded to commit suicide in order to 'leave their earthly containers and become more than human'. The idea of 'ascension', that a chosen few will survive the 'end of the world', runs through both the New Age and fundamentalist religions. However, in neither case are the chosen ones in a physical form, instead they survive as 'souls', or as 'higher beings', or 'on another planet in another dimension'!

Echoes of such beliefs have also been carried down into more mainstream self-help structures. Many of the self-development programmes today end up being 'self-repression' programmes. I personally have come across a number of positive thinking groups, which ultimately do not embrace the fullness of life and actually keep, people more 'in their heads' than ever! An over-emphasis on 'living in the light' easily ends up in denial of all that is human. Jealousy, anger, envy, lust, and other 'dark' traits may seem non-spiritual, but, in reality, trying to get rid of these lower emotions is just another ego-game. By denying these emotions, we also deny our positive animal nature, our instinct, sexuality, creativity and power.

Resistance is not the answer, neither is avoidance. The spiritual search can easily take the form of escapism. Being 'out there' sometimes seems preferable to being 'right here'. Being cosmic and angelic may seem heavenly, but this is not the whole story and it just leads to more imbalance. Getting high without staying grounded ends up with just being spaced out.

Wholeness means embracing all of our selves. Only acceptance of both the dark and the light, the beast and the beauty, the human and the divine will make us whole.

Heaven and Earth are like two lost lovers, each one yearning for the other in order to make themselves whole again. Whilst Heaven is out there being all perfect, Earth has been left down below to stew in a melting pot of increasing greed and corruption. As capitalism and consumerism run rampant, life becomes increasingly meaningless and dispirited. Spirit without substance is cold and alone, whilst Matter without sacredness is dangerous.

It is only when Heaven and Earth are reunited that a real transformation can occur. When the physical becomes spiritualized then consciousness evolves. Change can only happen in the present moment, and right now we are physical beings in a physical world. By inviting Spirit into our bodies, we change the way we perceive reality, we expand our senses and so we honour ourselves and each other. By imbuing the Earth with Spirit, everything that exists becomes sacred and so we care for the world we live in. This is how real change happens – by being totally present here and now.

This is the great paradox of Spirit and Matter: it is only by being fully present in our physical reality that we can penetrate the veil of illusion and get in touch with our spiritual essence. By going deep into the nature of reality, we discover that form arises from the formless and goes back to the formless. In other words, Spirit pervades everything. Ultimately, Existence is indivisible. Unity is its underlying nature.

The truly spiritual life is encapsulated in the Zen saying: 'Be in this world but not of it'. In other words, be totally present in the material world, do not escape it by denying your physical nature nor by living in a fantasy world created by your mind. Enter fully into your life, give yourself totally, with full awareness, but recognize that you are not it. You are beyond it, your essence, your very basic nature is spiritual.

Spirituality needs to be brought into the marketplace, for what is the use of being spiritual if you cannot cope with the mundane reality of day-to-day existence? What is the use of being spiritual if you cannot enjoy being human? Osho, one of the greatest spiritual teachers of our times, talks of the birth of a 'New Man', the creation of a new consciousness for the twenty-first century. He calls this 'Zorba the Buddha':

> *The New Man will be earthy and divine, worldly and otherworldly. The New Man will accept his totality and he will live it without inner division, he will not be split … The New Man will be Zorba the Greek and he will also be Guatam the Buddha … He will be sensuous and spiritual – physical, utterly physical, in the body, in the senses, enjoying the body … and still a great consciousness, a great witnessing will be there.*

OSHO, *Autobiography of a Spiritually Incorrect Mystic*

As we move into the twenty-first century we need to recognize that our reality is urban. As the power of the telecommunications network, the spread of information technology and the speed of travel all increase, the world is becoming smaller and the urban-rural divide is shrinking. It is high time that the apparent contradiction between being spiritual and getting your hands dirty in the real world was resolved. It is easy to see the worlds of business and commerce as far-removed from the world of Spirit, and indeed for the most part, they have been! We can clench our fists and curse at the people who control global finances and the trickle-down to our purse strings, we can rant and rave at the greedy corporations that put profit above service, we can bury our heads in the sand when faced with the injustices of major manufacturers.

But damning, accusing, ignoring and escaping are not the answer. These are not transformative qualities. We need to bring awareness to these issues, not run away from them. Money is not evil – just how we use it. Money is simply energy: when it flows it creates a current, that is, currency. This energy can be used without awareness, in other words, accumulation, leading to greed and destruction. Alternatively, it can be used with awareness and so becomes a source of abundance and creativity. Used in the right way, money does indeed make the world go round! Business is not evil – just how we do it. Business is simply a transaction, an energy exchange. Without awareness, the transaction stems from fear and is unbalanced, it becomes a power game. But *with* awareness, business becomes a way of creating a community and helps to make the world a better place.

The increasing number of successful businesses that combine high-quality goods and services with the conservation of natural resources – such as Anita Roddick's Body Shop and the Belgian-based Ecover – show that capitalism and sustainability can be comfortable bedfellows. As Lynn Franks, author of *The SEED Handbook*, says sustainable is best described as 'a garden, organic and self-sufficient, as it uses and replaces its natural supplies.'

The challenge today is to traverse the worlds of Matter and Spirit. Unity, not separation, is the new consciousness paradigm. This is radical change. We can re-create our urban reality by inviting Spirit home to where it belongs: in the heart of Matter, that is, right where it matters! Like a long-lost lover returning to the arms of his beloved, Spirit can be embraced in the everyday physical reality. This is the creation of Heaven on Earth.

The End of Time

We stand at the edge of a new reality. Predictions abound of the end of one world and the creation of another. The Bible describes an apocalyptic vision in which a worldwide Armageddon is followed by Paradise on Earth. The Native Americans talk of a time of 'purification', which will herald in a new era of peace. In the Hindu tradition, it is said that we are now close to the end of the *Kali Yuga*, the age of destruction, and we are about to enter the *Sat Yuga*, the age of enlightenment. All New Age belief systems share this theme: from the return of the New Messiah to the Ascension into Light, from the rebirth of a New World to the dawning of the Age of Aquarius, it seems that change is inevitable.

Many forward-thinking scientists now support this view. Some have predicted that statistically we are poised at the threshold of a major evolutionary leap, probably as radical as the one from higher primates to *Homo sapiens* all those millions of years ago. Others suggest that we are in the midst of a huge paradigm shift, which will totally restructure the way we see reality. And yet others are finding evidence of the increasing likelihood of geographical changes, which will change the face of the world as we know it.

Whether this change happens externally (in other words, a cataclysmic earth change) or internally, (in other words, a radical change in mass consciousness) – or both – remains to be seen. Spiritual teachers such as Sri Aurobindo, Osho, Da Free John, Ishwara Maitreya and 'The Mother', have variously spoken of the 'Dawn of a New Man', the 'Birth of a New Species', and the 'Buddhas of the New Dawn'. If we look around us today, in our urban world, we can already see the seeds of this transformation. The pursuit of self-development and spiritual growth is more acceptable in mainstream society. More and more people are turning to spiritual disciplines to bring meaning to their lives. Yoga is now enjoying a high-profile popularity thanks to various pop-star devotees such as Madonna; Ayurveda is gradually becoming a household term as famous models give it their stamp of approval; Tantra is creeping in between the sheets of magazine covers; and meditation is even mentioned on the evening news as a way to deal with stress. It seems that as modern life gets more and more filled with things to do and have, we need to look elsewhere for the space to just 'be'.

As the pace of modern life keeps increasing, time seems to be disappearing into a black hole. 5,000 years ago, the Mayans prophesied the end of time. But this does not necessarily mean that the world will end: rather, it points to the end of the illusion of time as we move into the eternal Now. As time continues to speed up, there comes a point where time stands still. It is very much like when you spin faster and faster and eventually it is as if you are not moving at all, you are just the stillpoint in the centre. This is the pause, the gap, the space or emptiness. This is where all duality is transcended and you just are. This is being totally 'in the Now', this is 'dying to the present moment'.

It is at this point that consciousness can expand, that it can move to a higher frequency. This is the frequency of ecstasy, the place of unity, where we are at one with ourselves and with the world around us. Ecstasy is a state of grace, where magic happens because we are one with the power of the universe.

Ecstasy is the new consciousness.

Chapter 5

Expand into Ecstasy

> *The stars go on dancing and moving, and the trees and the
> birds and the oceans, the Sun and the Moon ... the whole
> of Nature is full of bliss, ecstatic.*

OSHO

Everything Is Energy

The whole of creation is made up of energy. From the stars in the sky to the
soil beneath our feet, from the air that we breathe to the blood in our veins,
we are all made up of the same stuff. The whole of Existence is
consciousness in a variety of manifestations. Everything, from an elephant to
an amoeba, from a mountain to an atom, has consciousness to one degree
or another. Where there is life, there is energy – and where there is energy,
there is consciousness.

Ancient cosmologies all describe life as an expression of consciousness, as
the great Oneness from which we have been created, the Void from which
we came and to which we shall return. Today, physicists at the cutting-edge
of the new scientific paradigm have also discovered that what appears to
be solid is actually a vibrating mass of energy. All that exists, even an
inanimate object such as a car or something without apparent substance
such as a thought, is made up of these vibrations of energy. The difference
between something that appears solid and something that is invisible is the

frequency of the vibration. The denser the thing, the slower the vibration; the lighter the thing, the faster the vibration. Energy is everywhere and everything is energy.

Ecstasy is the direct experience of this energy. Since we are also made up of this energy, we can gain a direct experience of it through our bodies. We may feel this energy as a tingle, a prickly sensation, a warm rush, a slight tremble, a feeling of lightness. This is energy moving. This movement of energy, this flow, is also called *prana* in the ancient traditions of India, in China it is called *chi*, and in Japan it is called *ki*: today, these terms have infiltrated our vocabulary and have become synonymous with **energy**. There are also energy channels in the body, a bit like roadways, where this energy can flow. These are called *nadis* in the Indian system and **meridians** in the Chinese: again, these are terms that are increasingly used in the West. And there are practical techniques for enhancing this flow. When these channels are open and the energy flow is high, energy expands, that is, moves up a vibratory level. This is experienced as ecstasy. And ecstasy is experienced in the body – where else do you feel bliss, joy, delight and rapture?

Ecstasy is an energy expansion. It is an expansion of consciousness. It is an expansion of the boundaries of the self. The word ecstasy comes from the Greek word *exstasis* which means 'to move beyond what is not moving' and its Latin root means 'to stand outside of oneself'. Another way of saying it is, to become bigger than your small self. Ecstasy is transcendence. It is going beyond who you think you are. In other words, it is ending the trance of your limited perception. Usually, we think of a trance as an altered state of consciousness, an unusual state of mind. Being in a trance implies being 'out there', 'not quite all here', being in a fantasy-world, it is something unreal.

However, it is perhaps more accurate to say that it is our everyday reality that is a trance. What we think of as real, is actually an illusion, a limited viewpoint.

Ecstasy is the expansion into a greater reality. It is an expansion of perception, an ability to see things as they really are. Ecstasy is, in fact, an expansion of the senses, an opening of the valves that filter out the information about the world. When we open up to the greater reality, our perception expands to include information from previously hidden levels of Existence.

For example, if you are walking through the woods on a Sunday afternoon and you are in your 'everyday' mode of perception, then you will see yourself as a somewhat solid mass of matter with a definite shape that ends at the surface of your skin. You will feel the weight of your legs as you lift them to take each step; you will hear the scrunch of the autumn leaves under your feet; and you will look at the gnarled dry trunk of a tree over there and the squirrels scurrying to get out of your way over here. You are separate from your environment, a well-defined 'thing' amongst a number of other well-defined 'things' all separated by empty space.

But if you move into a state of ecstasy – perhaps triggered by the way the sunlight is coming through the branches of the tree or perhaps your are high after a long run or perhaps you have just been deep in meditation – then your previously hard edges will have melted and you will feel yourself as a somewhat more fluid mass of matter. As you become aware of tingles and rushes of energy moving through your body, you experience yourself as an undulating mass of vibrations. Every step you take becomes an intense pleasure as gentle currents of energy course through your legs and the sound of the leaves are like tinkling bells. You feel light, as if you have wings, you are floating through a beautiful landscape. Colours are vibrant, bursting inside you with delight. You do not end where your skin ends, rather you extend outwards, connected to all that is here. You, the trees, the squirrels, the birds, the sunlight, the sky, the wind, you are all here together in the garden of life – you are all vibrating masses of energy.

The more you expand into ecstasy, the more subtle the energy realms become. If you are sensitive enough, you will feel the presence of the spirit of the trees or the birds. You may even feel like taking a few moments to commune in silence with a particular tree or bird that you feel strongly connected to. And if you listen carefully, this spirit being may have a message for you. Not so long ago, I was taking my usual two-hour walk through Hampstead Heath, deeply pondering a problem that was troubling me. As I walked up the hill, the sun hit the branches above me and I heard the sweet song of a bird, one that was unfamiliar to me. I looked up and there was a blue jay looking down at me. For a few minutes, we were locked in some kind of communication, an unspoken understanding. The next instant the bird was gone and I was left feeling deeply touched and filled with awe. I realized I now had the answer to my problem. As I continued to walk, I felt strong and powerful and safe.

If you keep on expanding, you may eventually experience a transcendence of your 'self'. You will experience Union with the One, Absolute Stillness. A number of years ago, I had just finished a particularly punishing run up a long steep hill in the heat of a Greek island. The sun was just about to set and, as I stopped to catch my breath, I was hit by a ray of sunlight that seemed to go straight through my heart. As the light exploded inside me, I felt myself dissolve into a million pieces and merge with the sun, the sea and the hills around me. I was filled with a presence so huge, so loving and so beautiful that I fell to my knees shaking with exhilaration and with tears of gratitude pouring down my face. In that moment, an emotional wound from a broken relationship was healed and when I got up I was at peace, at one with myself and my world.

This is a description of a true religious experience, a deeply personal and utterly direct experience of Source. I have had many of these, some more profound and mind-blowing than others, but each one a great blessing.

This is the way of the mystic.

The Mystic Way

The mystic seeks a private affair with God, an intimate connection with Source. The mystic's way is that of union, of surrender. The path of the mystic weaves through many cultures and many ages. Look beyond the diversity of spiritual traditions and you will find that there is a common thread, for there is only one truth – remember, all spiritual paths lead to the One. It is here, at the core, at the heart, of spirituality that the mystic is to be found.

Whenever I mention the word 'mystic', nine times out of 10, people think I am referring either to Christianity or to some ethereal woman with a crystal ball! It is true that some mystics have been Christians, such as St Teresa of Avila, St Francis of Assisi, Hildegard of Bingen and St Joan of Arc. But it is also true that these so-called Christians have been classified as heretics by the Church and have lived in isolation, away from the strictures of traditional organized religion. These mystics found union with God outside of religious dogma. To them, Christ was found in Christ-consciousness, an inner state of awakening, and was not a mythical figure to be worshipped.

Before the Catholic Church took control of God, even before the founders of Christianity laid down the law according to their own gospel, Christ was to be found in the path of Gnosticism. 'Gnosis' means 'direct knowledge of the divine' and the Gnostics were those who were in the most intimate contact with Christ, both with the man himself and with the inner state of Christ-consciousness. These men and women of gnosis kept their knowledge private, secret, shrouded in mystery, so as to protect themselves from the persecution of those with religious power. No wonder mysticism is seen as something mysterious! In fact, the truth is simple: God is available to each and every one of us – we do not need a spokesman to give us permission!

Jesus himself was a mystic – was he not found guilty of heresy? Jesus was a rebel who lived life to the full. Far from being the saintly ascetic, Jesus was a man of passion. There is some evidence that Mary Magdalene was both his confidante and his consort and that dance, music and celebration were fully embraced on the path to God. Christ's message was of love – and love cannot possibly be ascetic!

There are mystics in Islam too. At the heart of Islam is Sufism, the path of Blissful Union. To the Sufi, God is 'the Beloved', the lover into whose embrace all is surrendered. Dig a little deeper and you will also find the mystic on the Tantric path. Tantra is the root of both Buddhism and Hinduism.

In Tantra, the lover is the beloved and it is through union with the opposite sex that God is reached. Here, sexuality and spirituality are totally united, the ultimate marriage of Matter and Spirit.

Go back far enough and you will find that Shamanism is the Mother of all mystics. Shamanism is common to all ancient cultures throughout the whole world, from the Eskimos of Alaska to the Tungus of Siberia and from the Mestizo of Peru to the Sora of India. The Pagan traditions of Western Europe are also a part of this Shamanic culture. Contrary to its popular definition, Shamanism is not a religion: there is no dogma here. Shamanism always relies on the direct experience of Source. In Shamanism, the whole of physical reality is imbued with Spirit. This includes our bodies, Nature and the universe – the whole of creation.

Come back to more recent times and you will find Osho – the 'spiritually incorrect mystic'. Osho's vociferous non-adherence to any religious dogma had surely got him into a lot of trouble. Expelled from America and banned from most countries in the world, Osho was greatly misunderstood for he threatened the status quo. Beneath the razzmatazz, blatant opulence and apparent discrepancies in his conduct, his message was always the same:

> *I teach freedom. Now man has to destroy all kinds of bondage and he has to come out of all prisons – no more slavery. Man has to become individual. Man has to become rebellious ... Spiritual to me, simply means finding oneself. I never allowed anybody to do this work on my behalf – because nobody can do this work on your behalf; you have to do it yourself.*
>
> OSHO, *Autobiography of a Spiritually Incorrect Mystic*

57

Whatever outer form any of these traditions take, whatever mystery surrounds them, at their core, at their heart, they all have in common what are known as 'techniques of ecstasy'. These are ways of opening up the energy channels in the physical body so as to expand into ecstasy. These always include a ritual practice involving at least one of the following: sex, dance, music and breathing techniques. From the Pagan practices of Christ to the secret rituals of the Gnostics, from the intoxicating path of the whirling dervishes to the cosmic orgasm sought after by the *tantrikas*, and from the ecstatic rituals of Shamanic cultures to the 'active meditations' of Osho – all these use one or more often a combination of these activities.

The way of the mystic is the path of ecstasy – and **ecstasy is the frequency of the heart**. It is in the heart that Heaven and Earth unite.

Ecstasy Today

Today ecstasy is more likely to be recognized as a pill that has reached notoriety on the dance-floor of club culture as well as in the tabloid press. Before its use as a recreational drug, ecstasy, or MDMA, had been used by psychotherapists who discovered that its primary effect was to 'open the heart'. Labelled by the scientific community as an 'empathogen', it was seen to enhance the ability to feel empathy and to aid clear and honest communication without the usual ego-defences.

And for a time, this substance indeed captured the hearts of a generation! The mass production and popularization of ecstasy has certainly been in keeping with the spiritual zeitgeist. The 'caring, sharing 90s' was a time when we collectively sought to heal our emotional wounds, a time when we yearned for some kind of community with the brotherhood and sisterhood of humanity. What better time to explore the realm of the heart?

It is no secret that people of all ages, backgrounds and social status have at one time or another tried ecstasy, both throughout the UK and the US as well as across Europe. A few years ago, I held a joint symposium with Nicholas Saunders (author of *E for Ecstasy* and co-author of *In Search of the Ultimate High: Spiritual Uses of Psychoactives*) and Julia Franks (a psychotherapist). We were exploring the potential for ecstasy to provide a spiritual awakening. And we had collated evidence that, for some people, a doorway to freedom had indeed been accessed. For some, 'getting out of their heads' had enabled them to tap into new sources of creativity and vision, which they were then able to bring back to their daily lives. For others, the pure joy of being able to experience a heart-connection with others had helped them to overcome mild depression. And in yet other cases, their experience of ecstasy had turned them on to a more traditional spiritual path. There are several accounts, too, of monks from various traditional disciplines who had tried ecstasy and drew parallels with the state of meditation.

It does not matter whether ecstasy comes in the form of a psychoactive or in the form of sex, dance, chanting, drumming, breathing, or anything else. All of these have been and are still used as keys to ecstasy. But this is all that they are – just the keys, not the ecstasy itself! This is an important point as there is much misunderstanding, especially in the case of psychoactives. And since we live in an urban world where we cannot possibly deny that recreational drug use is a part of our society, this needs some clarification.

Psychoactives have been taken as keys to spiritual awakening for millennia, but always in a formalized setting. To the Naga Saddhus of India, marijuana is the 'sacred grass' of Shiva; to the Rastafarians of Jamaica, ganja is the 'holy herb'; and to the Huichol of Mexico, the peyote mushroom is the 'Grandfather' who shows the 'right way of living'. In West Africa, the Bwiti religion involves lengthy initiation rites with the use of the root bark ibogaine. And in Brazil, the jungle vine *ayahuasca* is regularly used in religious services by both indigenous and urban peoples. In particular, the *Santo Daime* and the *Uniao do Vegetal* are well-established churches that combine Nature Spirituality with a hefty dose of Christianity, and with *ayahuasca* as the sacrament. Its use in this way has been shown to reduce the incidence of drug addiction and violence in inner cities and to bring a sense of meaning and sacredness into daily urban life.

In this context, these practices have been aptly called 'technologies of the sacred'. But – and it is a big BUT – taken out of this context, they lose their sacredness, they lose their meaningfulness. Yes, in the right person at the right time, recreational use may spark off a spiritual awakening, but in general it is a hit-and-miss affair. It is a little like opening Pandora's box: you do not know whether you will encounter angels or monsters, you do not know if you will ascend to Heaven or descend to Hell – and without a map you will surely get lost! Scientific research has shown time and time again that the set and setting are vital to the outcome of a psychoactive session: in other words, it is the **purpose** and **context** that are important. Just like any other spiritual path – whether it be meditation, fasting, Pagan ritual or Shamanic practice – you must prepare for the journey.

Whilst recreational drug use is an unconscious urge for transcendence, a yearning for freedom, it is exactly that – **unconscious**! The trend for 'mix and match', getting 'completely out of it' and doing it as often as possible is a recipe for disaster. The psychological and physiological price to pay is too high. Without awareness, 'teacher medicines' are reduced to just a bunch of chemicals. Without sacredness, psychoactive use – and you could substitute sex, dance, or anything else here – is just a form, devoid of meaning and ultimately alienating to the soul.

My first taste of ecstasy was in the form of a pill; but I already had an intensive background in psychology, a strong enquiring mind and a latent urge to experience the deeper mystery of life. My set and setting had provided me with the opportunity for a spiritual awakening and the time, for me, was ripe! I was also aware somehow, that whatever experience we have, whatever the apparent external cause of it, it is always because that experience is actually within us.

The seed of my work was inspired by my desire to create natural ways of experiencing ecstasy. Ecstasy is something natural; it is a state of being that we can all contact. It is just that we have forgotten how. My work has been the creation of 'techniques of ecstasy', techniques to open your energy channels, so that you too can find the mystic within.

The Ultimate Orgasm

Ecstasy is the experience of an expansion into the Now. Expansion can only happen in the Now: the past and the future are limited, finite events. They are captured moments, frozen in time. But the present moment, the Now, is beyond time. It is limitless, infinite, eternal. Transcendence, going beyond, can only happen in the Now!

This is the true meaning of Tantra. Tantra means 'to expand' (from the Sanskrit word *tan*). Tantra is not sex, even though that is how the media and popular culture like to portray it. It is not even 'spiritual sex'. How can sex be spiritual? Sex is simply sex! However, you can bring awareness to the sexual act. By bringing awareness continuously into the present moment, you can get in touch with the energy flow during sex. If the energy channels are clear and the energy flow expands, consciousness also expands.

This is Tantra: the experience of this expansion. Everything else, the convoluted positions, the special breathing techniques, the meditations and rituals, are simply Tantric techniques of ecstasy. All these are designed to heighten your awareness, to bring you more and more into the present moment, to open your energy channels and to elevate a purely physical act to a sacred one. Tantra is not the technique, the structure, it is not the form: it is the formless that is reached through the form.

The true meaning of Tantra is transcendence through the union of opposites, the union of yin and yang, male and female, Matter and Spirit, sacred and profane. Tantra is the absolute surrender to the reality of Now. In Tantra, there is no resistance, no avoidance: every moment is experienced as fully as possible, life is lived totally! There is no 'No' in Tantra, only 'Yes!' Whatever is encountered in life, whatever obstacle, difficulty or discomfort, whatever pleasure, delight or titillation, it is fully embraced with total awareness. It is all very well learning Tantric techniques for sex or whatever, but if you then spend the rest of your time denying certain parts of yourself or judging other people's behaviour, then you are not truly on the Tantric path. The Tantric path is really the cultivation of an attitude towards life: an attitude of surrender, of union.

If you keep on saying 'Yes' to life, life will keep on stretching your edges until you come up against your boundaries, your discomfort zone. This is the threshold, the 'limen', the line between the known and the unknown. This is the place of expansion, the place of growth.

My teaching is Tantric. I may provide the techniques for ecstasy, but what I am really doing is pushing you to the edge of surrender. I find that for most of us Westerners this surrender is very difficult. Much of what I teach is formless, it is more about bringing awareness to your own energy flow. But the mind, especially the 'highly civilized' urban mind, loves form, structure, routine, logical sequences to follow. Then the mind is happy, it can just mindlessly do what it is being told. To surrender, though, requires awareness. It also requires trust. To let go is to step into the unknown. In this place of 'let-go' there is nothing to do and this feels scary! The place of being is unfamiliar. It is always fresh, new, alive: otherwise it would be known and what is known is stagnant. Being requires vulnerability, the ability to take a risk. It requires courage to step into the unknown.

Surrender will bring liberation, it will lighten the load. But it will also drop you to your depths. It is like dancing on the edge, the edge between dark and light, the edge between Heaven and Hell. A dance is a play of energies, a push and a pull, an up and a down. Ultimately, this is all that life is: a dance between polarities. This is Tantra: simply a surrender to what is.

It is not Tantric sex but more like a Tantric dance. Anyway, sex, dance ... it is all the same, for what is sex if not a dance between opposites?

Tantra is union with all of life, the whole of Existence. It is the ultimate orgasm, the ultimate ecstasy!

2: The Preparation

You are just getting in tune. It is like … if you have seen Indian classical musicians playing … for half an hour, or sometimes more, they simply go on fixing their instruments. They will move their knobs, they will make the strings tight or loose, and the drum player will go on checking his drum – whether it is perfect or not. For half an hour they go on doing this. This is not music, this is just preparation.

OSHO

The Preparation

Chapter 6

Come Into Your Body

The only thing we really have is nowness, is now.

SOGYAL RINPOCHE

Now Is All There Is

NOW is the only reality. It is the only reality that **matters**. In other words, it is through the direct contact with our material nature – in other words, the body – that we access the present moment. To put it even more simply, being in the body is being here and now. The past is merely a memory and the future is just a fantasy – **only the present moment is real**. By being fully present in the body, you get in touch with reality.

To touch something is to feel it, to experience its essence. And you can only do this if you enter this something fully. In other words, when you bring total awareness to your body, you will start to feel it from within. Now you start to drop the concept of body (two arms, two legs, a torso, a head, skin, etc.). Now the body is no longer a visible, solid mass: this is just the outer shell, just a particular perception from a particular point of view. As you bring more and more awareness to the body, you start to penetrate its deeper reality. This is the **inner body**, the invisible, indivisible energy field that permeates your whole being. As you start to get in touch with this, every cell of your body will feel alive and vibrant. As you go deeper, you will experience more and more subtle energy fields until you move beyond the form, beyond the physical, and into the formless. Now you are in touch with your essence, the essence of Existence. This is a state of pure awareness, a state of being. This is the infinite, eternal Now.

This is what the 'new physicists' call the 'quantum reality'. Here, there are only 'quantums', packets of energy with the potential to appear as Matter. In fact, what seems solid is instead a mass of vibrating energy. And what seems like empty space is actually full of 'quantum energy fields'. These quantum fields lie at the edge of time and space, at the edge of form and formless. And beyond this quantum reality is what physicists have called the 'unified field', the ultimate reality that lies beneath everything … the place of pure potential, the Source.

This unified reality is always here, there and everywhere. It always has been and always will be. But we are mostly unaware of its existence. The most direct way to get in touch with it is through the body. By bringing awareness to the body, we enter more deeply into the true nature of Existence. This is another one of those great paradoxes of life: by fully entering the material world, you experience the spiritual.

Your body is like a gateway. It is through this gateway that we access our multi-dimensional nature. We are physical, emotional, mental and spiritual beings. These levels exist simultaneously, all at once, all the time. The place where these levels meet, the interface between form and formless, is where we can get in touch with the body's innate intelligence. Deepak Chopra – renowned medical doctor and spiritual teacher – calls this the **quantum**

body. It is here that thoughts become emotions and emotions become physical symptoms: it is here that mind and body are one. This is the place where wellness – or illness – is created: this is the place of healing.

It is from this place that seemingly miraculous cures happen. There are many reported – and probably a lot more unreported – stories of people who have fully recovered from fatal diseases even though traditional medical intervention had failed to help. Amongst the most well-known are those of Louise Hay and Brandon Bays, both of whom totally healed themselves of terminal cancer through the transformation of negative emotional and thought patterns. Both of these remarkable women are now high-profile workshop leaders and authors, helping countless others on the road to self-healing.

Personally, I shall never forget the 75-year-old woman I met at a 'healing dance' class several years ago. She had been diagnosed with an advanced stage of cancer and given only a few months to live. The extensive radiation treatment she had been subjected to had no effect other than to cause all her hair to fall out. So she had stopped all medical treatment and had given up. Well, after a few months she had gone back to the doctors and her tests had shown no sign of cancer at all! I looked at this lively woman, whose eyes sparkled and who danced with all the elegance and sprightliness of a young nymph, and asked her how she did it. She told me she had just gone deep into herself through silence and solitude and found the root cause of her disease. She had been frightened of death and so she had frightened herself to death! When she fully faced this fear by making it conscious, the disease was released.

Deepak Chopra also cites numerous examples of fatal illnesses going into spontaneous remission in response to a variety of alternative treatments, from special diets to super-vitamin therapy and from positive thinking to prayer. When this phenomenon was looked into more closely, it was found that what all these had in common was a point at which the patients saw their illness as illusory. In other words, they knew with certainty that their underlying nature was whole and healthy. What all these cases actually have in common is that the people in question were able to get in touch with their quantum body.

Increasingly, medical science is recognizing the inherent power of the body-mind link. The first clear-cut evidence of this appeared in the 1980s when a medical doctor found that advanced stages of coronary heart disease could be completely reversed with alternative treatment methods, namely a combination of meditation, visualization, hands-on energy healing and prayer. More recently, scientists have discovered that there is a closed circuit between the brain and the body's immune system: when the brain hemispheres are out of synch – as they frequently are in our everyday mode of thinking – then the balance of the immune system is upset. This relatively new field of 'psychoneuroimmunology' has also revealed that there are biochemical units of emotion, which play a vital role in the function of the body's defence system. It all makes sense really when you consider the power of 'being here now'.

Today, a number of well-respected doctors are recognizing that the traditional medical model needs to extend itself to include the anatomy of the spirit. Carolyn Myss, a 'medical intuitive', has done much to demythologize the more esoteric causes of illness by collaborating closely with several conventional doctors over the years. Her work has created a model of the human energy system that truly traverses both orthodox and alternative schools of thought. As science delves deeper into the nature of reality, the boundaries between biology and biography are increasingly becoming blurred. As the quantum nature of matter is revealed, so the 'quantum body' is seen to be the underlying structure that governs our health.

The quantum body is our life force, otherwise known as *prana, chi* or *ki*. We activate its power – in other words, its potential for well-being – through **awareness**. Spiritual disciplines from the East that include body-mind practices, such as yoga, t'ai chi, chi kung and aikido, all have this understanding at their core. They all activate the healing power of our innate life force by bringing awareness to the quantum body. They all utilize the gateway of the physical body to access our multi-dimensional nature. It is for this reason that these practices are so potent in rebalancing body, mind and spirit. Not only do they boost the immune system, have an anti-ageing effect on the body's cellular structure and greatly enhance energy levels, but they also calm the emotions, relax the mind and awaken the spirit.

Other Eastern healing disciplines, such as acupuncture, shiatsu and reiki, also utilize the power of *prana/chi*. In the West, *prana/chi* has been called 'subtle energy', 'vital force', 'bioplasma', 'orgone energy' and 'biomagnetic field'. It is also more commonly known as the 'aura', which clairvoyants and healers are able to see as well as it being observed with Kirlian photography. Several scientific studies have tapped into this energy via the body's electromagnetic field and have used electromagnetic therapy to successfully treat physical and psychological illness. Western holistic therapies, such as reflexology, holistic massage and hands-on healing, also tap into this energy.

Prana/chi is simply **awareness in motion**. Movement is life and stagnation is death. When *prana/chi* flows freely through all our levels, we are healthy, wholesome, complete. When *prana/chi* is stuck, then we are *dis*-eased, unwholesome, incomplete. Stagnation or 'stuckness' is not the same as stillness. Stillness is what lies beneath the movement. Stillness is pure awareness, the Source. As humans, we cannot be totally at this stillpoint. This is the place where Spirit is alone; there is no life here, only potential for life. Life itself is movement. However, as humans, we can be both in stillness and in motion at the same time. It is at this edge between form and formless, where one is contained within the other, that we can transcend the purely physical and experience the spiritual.

It is at this edge that we expand our awareness, that we move beyond our limited perception of how things are. It is here that we lose our sense of separation, which is ultimately the root cause of all our disease and distress. Here, we transcend duality, we go beyond life and death and connect to the greater reality. This place is limitless and timeless and therefore fearless and deathless. This is the place of enlightenment.

● ●

This little exercise gets you in touch with your inner body or quantum body. It only takes a few minutes and can be done anytime and anywhere. With practice, you can keep tapping into this energy whenever you need to: for instance, when you are tired and low in energy, when you are stressed out and have a head full of worrying thoughts, when you feel a little run down and maybe have a cold coming on, just before an important meeting, and so on.

Touch Your Essence

For now just sit or lie down comfortably and close your eyes.

Simply decide to bring your awareness, the focus of your attention, to your body. Become aware of your feet, legs, abdomen, chest, arms, hands, head. Spend a few moments with each part of the body just feeling it. The more attention you give to feeling it, the more you will feel. If you find yourself thinking about it, just bring your focus back to feeling the body. You may find yourself getting a sense of warmth in the body or a tingling or some other sensation – this is great, just keep focusing on it!

Now allow yourself to be aware of your whole body. Can you feel the subtle energy field that pervades your inner body? As your awareness moves deeper into your inner body, you will go beyond feeling just physical sensations to feeling something more subtle.

With practice, as you keep your awareness here for longer, the feeling will become stronger and you may feel your cells vibrating, coming alive. After a while you may feel your body becoming translucent, as if you are glowing, as if you are made of light – this is great, now you are in touch with your essence!

(ADAPTED FROM ECKHART TOLLE, *The Power of Now*)

● ●

The Body Is Your Map

The body is a bridge between Heaven and Earth. It is the playground of your soul, that part of your spiritual essence that comes to experience life in the earthly dimension. It is through the body that you sense, feel and process your experiences. It is through your body that you interact with your environment and express your soul's purpose. The body is simply a vehicle for the soul. And just like any mode of transport, its function is to provide movement. And where there is movement, there is life.

The body is a navigational tool. It is a map to guide you through life. The soul speaks through your sensations, feelings, thoughts and emotions. These are the indicators on the map and all these are experienced and expressed through the gateway of your body. It is your body that instinctively knows when something feels right or whether it feels wrong. It is your body that tenses up as a warning of danger, that tingles with excitement, that is flooded with waves of bliss. And it is your body that weakens and slows down when things are just too much to handle, that gets inflamed with rage, that burns with passion, that has a spring in its step when things are going well, that glows with an inner smile when life is good.

The body is a map of your story. Your past, present and future are all encoded here. Every cell holds an imprint of everything you have experienced since birth. Every painful memory, every trauma, every unresolved issue, all these leave an indelible mark. Every moment of joy, delight, happiness and bliss, all these are recorded here. Your habitual responses to life, your attitudes, your state of wellness or illness, all these can be understood by reading the map of your body. Every bump, lump, line and wrinkle tells the story of your past. The shape and size of every part of you, the way you move, the way you sit, the way your body parts interact with each other, all these show how you experience life in the present. And at a quantum level, your body holds the seeds of your future: here is your potential for change.

Whole systems of body-mind therapies are based on this understanding. In Ayurveda, that most ancient of systems from India, mind and body go hand in hand in creating health and life attitudes. Here, physiological and psychological characteristics are closely linked, giving rise to a number of body types with specific predisposition to certain illnesses as well as specific personality traits. In Chinese medicine too, physical and psychological constitution are linked to lifestyle and well-being.

Here in the West, the psychologist Wilhelm Reich was the first to introduce the idea that the outer body is related to the inner life. Reich believed that a person who shows physical signs of imbalance, inflexibility and weakness, will also exhibit these characteristics in their personality. To Reich, the body's sexual functioning was the absolute measure of well-being on all levels. He believed that when the body-mind is healthy – in other words, when energy is flowing freely through the physical, emotional and mental levels – then 'orgiastic potency', as he called it, is also healthy. Reich believed (and quite rightly so!) that the ability to have a full body orgasm is a reflection of how truly alive and conscious someone is. I would say that this is in complete agreement with the Tantric approach. In Tantra, full body orgasm is achieved by opening the energy channels of the body and this leads to the awakening of consciousness. Tragically, Reich was imprisoned for his 'radical' views – it was, after all, the era of repression and depression.

But his work spawned a whole host of body-mind therapies, which now make up the backbone of the Human Potential movement.

Most prominently, these include Rolfing, Feldenkreis, and Bionergetics. In Rolfing, emotional blocks are released through deep tissue manipulation, for it is here deep in the fascial tissues of the body that emotional rigidity sets in. In Feldenkreis, neuromuscular co-ordination is the key to healthy self-image and self-awareness, so that the way we move and hold ourselves reflects how we see ourselves. And in Bioenergetics, psychological well-being is achieved through the physical, emotional and intellectual treatment of 'body expression', i.e. the postures we adopt in life. Other therapies, such as Gestalt, encounter, primal and psychodrama, are offshoots of Reich's work. Even something as apparently unrelated as the '5Rhythms' method developed by Gabrielle Roth where dance is the vehicle for psycho-emotional exploration, is also a part of this family of body-mind systems. And even more on the outskirts than this, Barbara Ann Brennan – the healer with 'hands of light' – has developed a whole system, which links subtle energy fields with physical, emotional, mental and spiritual self-expression.

What all these ancient and modern systems are really saying, is that we each have a unique story to tell and any self-respecting wise-woman or man will affirm that story-telling is a powerful initiation. By telling our story, we unravel our personal history and we reveal who we are. By telling our story, we step into the power of the present moment and open ourselves up to the power of healing. Our story can be told not only in words but also through our physical expression. Every gesture, every posture, every stance we take, every step we make – all these speak volumes about where we have come from, who we think we are and who we are becoming.

Through awareness and movement, you can get in touch with your story and start to move beyond your limitations. As you get in touch with the inner flow of life-force, you start to create an inner expansion. With this expansion comes inner space and silence in which to experience the Now. Movement and change can only happen in the present moment, in the Now. This is the place of expansiveness and freedom, the place of potential and possibilities. Here, in the space and silence, the emptiness, there is room for growth. Here, you become like an empty vessel, waiting to be filled by Spirit. It is the power of Spirit that moves you. Like the 'winds of change', when Spirit flows through you, there is a great cleansing, a great healing. By taking your awareness deep into your body, you open the door to the transformative power of Spirit. **The power of change is always in the present**. Your body is a doorway, a portal to the **power of Now**.

To truly understand what this means is part of the journey of being human, the journey back to wholeness. So many of us live in our heads, looking for something 'out there' to bring meaning to our existence. So many of us live cut off from our bodies: we may feed them, clothe them, even pamper them from time to time, but do we truly feel them? If we did, we would realize that the body is the abode of the soul. So many of us externalize the search for Spirit, as if it is something outside of ourselves. But the search stops right here, right now! There is nowhere to go but **in**!

I always remember the time I met Foster Perry, the gifted healer, Shaman and story-teller. I had been on the spiritual path for several years and thought of myself as pretty sorted on cosmic matters. At this particular workshop, Perry spent a long while with each participant, taking them back to relive past-lives in graphic detail. There was a great deal of cathartic transformation as incredible stories were revealed and old traumas were released. I waited my turn expectantly. Finally, he turned to me and simply said loudly: 'GET YOUR SOUL BACK IN YOUR BODY!' Then he tapped me really hard on the crown of my head and turned away. I was shocked and dismayed! How could he dismiss me with such a shallow statement?

It has taken me many more years of soul-searching to truly understand the profundity of this simple teaching he gave me. The power of my healing resides in the present moment, in being fully present. It is here and now that body and Spirit exist in wholeness – there is nothing else to know.

My motto today is **GET OUT OF YOUR HEAD AND INTO YOUR BODY**: your body is a gift, a gateway to the Divine – so get into it!

● ●

This exercise is an extension of 'Touch Your Essence' – it is something to do, perhaps for half an hour, as a form of meditation, or just before you go to sleep is a great time. This exercise will take you deep into your quantum body and works to clear negativity, boost your immune system and prolong longevity:

Explore the Edge

Sit or lie comfortably with your eyes closed and take a few moments to get in touch with your breath, just watching it rise and fall in the body – there should be no great effort here, stay relaxed but focussed.

Bring your awareness to your feet, just feeling them. Direct your breath here – imagine the feet are actually breathing. Now become aware of the edge between the skin on your feet and the space surrounding them ... become aware of the minutest sensations such as changes in temperature, tingling, itching, etc. Now move your attention inside the feet and stay aware of the sensations – you may get inner impressions such as feelings of lightness or heaviness or even different colours, or you may start feeling an emotion such as anger or sadness. Keep moving your attention deeper into the essence of feet – keep exploring the edge of form and formless.

If an uncomfortable sensation arises or your inner impression is a dark one, take a deep intentional breath and direct it to this area, then exhale fully so that you release this negativity/pain/darkness on the out-breath. Keep doing this until the area feels clear and light. Now as you breathe in you can imagine drawing in golden light on the in-breath and letting this permeate the whole area you are working on.

Repeat this process (it gets easier with practice!) with each body part; be as thorough as you can.

Now just spend a few moments breathing golden light into the whole of your body. Watch as the boundaries between inner and outer dissolve – you have expanded your edge!

● ●

Chapter 7

Empty Your Vessel

If you want to get a full day of satisfying life, you must empty yourself, mind, heart, bowels, and to some extent, even your wallet, on a daily basis.

BAREFOOT DOCTOR

So Full!

To empty your vessel is to prepare for God. Only an empty cup can be filled with the light of Spirit. As human beings, we do not come into this world empty. Simply having a physical body means that density is our most basic nature – and density is the opposite of emptiness.

The mere act of being born means that we already imprint intense pain – and pleasure – into our cellular memory. In fact, our life patterns are directly linked to this birth trauma. How we respond to the ups and downs of life is a mirror of how we experienced the life and death struggle of our birth process. Contrary to the opinion of some psychologists, we do not come into this world as a *tabula rasa*: we are not a blank slate that is shaped solely by what we learn from our environment. Our entry into this life has already created a blueprint for the most poignant, primal and profound feelings and emotions we will ever have. Stan Grof goes even further, linking current life patterns with past-life imprints. His extensive research points to the existence of 'karmic patterns', which replay themselves as lessons to be learnt in this lifetime and which are also replicated in the birth process.

The whole of life's journey is a replaying or unravelling of these imprints. By replaying them, we have the opportunity to make them more conscious. In other words, by experiencing our pain, our blocks, we have the opportunity to bring them out of density – that is, out of where they are stuck in cellular memory – and into the light of awareness where they can dissolve. The whole of life is simply a preparation for enlightenment. The soul's ultimate purpose is enlightenment – merging with the One/Source/God. Life is a journey back to Source. Only with the passage through earthly life can the soul undertake this journey. Every experience we have, every bump, bruise, knock and scratch, is simply an opportunity to get closer to God. We have two choices. We can either resist, withdraw, suppress: in other words we can hold onto our 'shit', our pain. Or we can embrace, accept, surrender: in other words, we can let go. The former makes us denser, the latter makes us lighter. All the stresses and strains, traumas and dramas of life are here to teach us one thing: how to let go. Letting go creates the space, the emptiness that allows Spirit to enter. Preparation means learning the tools for letting go. All spiritual practices that have developed over the ages are, in fact, **methods of letting go**. These practices provide the tools that prepare us for the journey back to God.

Today, we face the greatest challenge in our collective evolutionary story so far. Through the passage of time and the increasing complexities of the modern age, we have accumulated so much density that letting go is an imperative if we are to survive. As the modern world moves away from its natural roots, so spiritual wisdom is lost – and so are the tools. Education, religion, politics and economics – all man-made constructs – have conspired to hide the truth. Through fear and ignorance, we are holding on for dear life. But holding on is killing us! It is now a 'do or die' situation. Either we wake up, learn to let go and release ourselves from our own bondage, or else we keep holding on, live in limitation and suffer.

The urban lifestyle encourages us to be human 'doings'. Our lives are filled with doing this and doing that, endlessly trying to keep on top of things. The modern urban person is increasingly self-sufficient, having to contend with a multiplicity of tasks. These days, there is so much more information to deal with: mobile phones, land lines, emails, Internet, newspapers, magazines, advertising … the array is startling. There is so much new technology to master: computers, digital cameras, on-line TVs, CD-ROMs, DVDs, WAP phones, MP3 players … hi-tech gadgets are proliferating. The entertainment industry too has exploded: we can now amuse ourselves with a mind-boggling selection of TV programmes, videos and DVDs to suit our mood from the leisure of our own homes; we can escape into a fantasy world at the 'big screen'; we can dance the night away in clubs, drink ourselves into oblivion in bars, titillate our taste buds with exotic food from all around the globe; and we can travel to the ends of the world in almost the blink of an eye. We can now 'shop till we drop': we shop for relaxation and recreation; we shop for the basic necessities because we have to and we shop for the luxuries because we want to; we shop when we're down to cheer ourselves up and we shop when we're high because it's a buzz! On top of it all, for many of us, there are creative business projects to run, families to cater for, friendships to nurture, homes to decorate, and traffic to contend with. Our days are filled with things to watch, things to read, things to think about, things to do and things to have. No wonder there is little room left for God!

Junk Is Stress

Just like the machine of consumerism that creates more and more toxic waste as a by-product, so do we create more and more junk within ourselves as we seek to consume the modern world. This junk is the equally toxic build-up that we have so much difficulty letting go of. Another word for this is stress.

Stress is the biggest killer around. Stress destroys health and erodes happiness, it eats away at life-force. It is only in the last 20 years that stress has become a mainstream concept. In the early 1980s, when I was researching the effects of stress on body-mind health, we academics were still struggling with the definition of stress. Up until then, stress was something that happened to a piece of metal when a very heavy load was applied to it. I remember writing a short article on my research in the first UK health magazine, called *Workout*. Such was the media response to this article that I shot to rapid fame as a 'stress and health' expert. The next few years were busy ones for me, writing magazine articles, running seminars, presenting at conferences, and being interviewed for TV programmes.

Today, stress is a part of our normal vocabulary and a part of our everyday reality. Not only is there the ever-increasing stress of financial pressure, job satisfaction, career competition, broken relationships and single parenthood, but there is also the stress of urban over-crowding and over-consumption. Today, we get stressed commuting to and from work, stressed sitting at our desks all day, stressed standing in queues, stressed waiting for the lights to change from red to green, stressed keeping up with everything. There is no doubt about it, modern life is stressful!

Stress affects every aspect of our being – the physical, emotional, mental and spiritual – for these are all connected at the quantum level. Stress is what happens when we overload our system. When we are stressed the flow of life-force gets interrupted, an imbalance is created, we function less than optimally and eventually the system starts to break down. When we suffer from stress, we cannot cope, we feel run down, we are low in energy. Eventually we get ill, disease sets in and we find ourselves creeping towards old age faster than we'd like.

Stress is simply stuck energy – and, like anything that is stuck, this energy eventually stagnates and pollutes. This is the 'junk' that we carry around – in our bodies, in our emotions, in our minds. And in the fast-paced world of the modern urban jungle we are mass-producing it! At every level that we assimilate life, we are producing junk as a by-product. And since every level is connected to the other levels, the effect is contagious.

On a physical level, what we take in through our mouths and into our stomachs is a reflection of how we digest life. Junk food is one of the main culprits when it comes to the toxins we accumulate. It makes sense, for 'we are what we eat'! We may eat more than our fair share in the West, but we certainly are not well nourished! Food stripped of its nutritional value – as in fast food, refined foods, frozen foods, processed foods, etc. – is highly imbalanced and therefore creates an imbalance in our bodies. Artificial colourings, flavourings, preservatives and pesticides, all these create unnatural by-products. As our bodies struggle to deal with this onslaught of chemicals, toxins accumulate in our fatty cells and our digestion becomes impaired. Over time, we suffer from fatigue, mood swings, obesity, irritable bowel syndrome, constipation, diabetes and coronary heart disease. It is clear that fast foods speed up the ageing process!

As fast as we are with our eating habits, we are terribly slow in another respect. As civilization has progressed, we have become increasingly sedentary. The invention of the chair has been responsible for more spinal imbalances than any other instrument. Backache is now a major complaint in the Western world and one of the main reasons for taking time off work. Repetitive Strain Injury is on the rise as we force the body to perform increasingly complex and tiny movements to match our increasingly complex and tiny technology. In the urban world, there is little room to bend, sway, flex and squat. Instead, we sit, slouch and slob. Lack of movement and insufficiently consistent physical exertion means that the body does not function optimally. Without free-flowing movement, there is no free-flowing energy and so we get ill. Obesity, osteoporosis, high blood pressure, coronary heart disease and depression, all these are the result of sluggishness.

Just as energy needs to flow on a physical level, so we need to create space for the free flow of our emotions. The modern urban lifestyle leaves little room for this. Thousands of years of suppression of the wild, chaotic part of us has led to a deep repression of our more primal emotions. The more civilized we have become, the more we have learnt to repress ourselves. Children are to be 'seen and not heard', 'big boys don't cry', and a 'stiff upper lip' is a sign of good upbringing. At school we are taught to behave, to 'be nice', to watch our 'Ps and Qs'. As adults, we put on a 'brave face', 'keep a lid on things' and hide the way we feel. Not only do we not easily air our true feelings, but there is also little breathing space in which to give vent to all our emotions. In the urban landscape, where can we go to scream, cry, jump and stomp? If we ever do give ourselves permission to let go, we are labelled 'crazy'.

In the urban world, there is little space or time for the sharing of unexpressed emotions, hidden issues and personal problems. In the busy-ness of our daily schedules, the anonymity of the big city and the hierarchical structure of modern society, we have lost the skill of sharing from the heart. Whereas in tribal communities everyone would come together to voice grievances, concerns, fears, hopes, dreams, gratitudes and blessings, today some of us pay huge sums of money to come together in a 'sharing circle'. And even then, it is most often outside the context of our immediate day-to-day social environment.

The skills of communicating and communing have been lost. If anything remotely uncomfortable arises, it is held in, pushed down, shoved aside, until it festers and eats away from the inside. Guilt, shame, repressed anger, unresolved sadness, all these lead to psychological and physical illness. Frequently, all this suppressed energy can no longer be held in, and just like a pot that has reached boiling point, the lid is expelled and the poison bursts out uncontrollably. When rage erupts it is most often taken out on those closest to us: wives, husbands, girlfriends, boyfriends, children and pets. The increasing divorce rates, physical and emotional violence in families, sexual abuse of children and cruelty to animals is a testament to this.

Most of us run away from our deeper feelings, just as we are constantly on the run in our busy lives. The 'work-shop-socialize' syndrome is an urban phenomenon and there is little room for silence. Information overload, noise pollution, over-stuffed filofaxes, deadlines that should have been met yesterday and social arrangements planned for tomorrow ... our heads spin with mental over-stimulation. Without time-out, our thoughts run rampant, going round and round in our heads with no space to just 'be'. The modern world provides us with too many choices, too many decisions to be made and we just end up with our nerves frayed, feeling tired and anxious.

We are so full of junk that we cannot sense the presence of our soul. Insight, intuition, vision and purpose are all hidden beneath layers of stress. We are alienated, disconnected, out of touch with who we are. When life is without meaning and direction, then confusion and apathy are common complaints. The alarming and escalating incidence of violence and drug abuse within ever-younger generations is clearly a symptom of the nihilism that results from a life devoid of spirituality. When we are disconnected from Spirit, then we are disconnected from the self – and when we disconnect from ourselves, then we disconnect from everyone else around us. The result is a loss of community.

Stress is what happens when we have no way of clearing this junk. It is not so much what comes at us from the outside but rather how we deal with it. It is our perception and our response that matters. Extensive animal and human studies have shown that when the subjects have some degree of control over the stressful stimulus, they suffer less than when they are helpless, even if the stressor is more intense. Other studies have shown that if subjects are given an outlet for feelings of frustration, then the harmful effects of the stressor are diminished. It seems that it is how we cope with stress that matters.

In other words, **we need to develop tools in order to empty our vessel**. We clearly need to let go of our junk, we need to clean up, we need a catharsis. And we need this on all three levels of our 'vessel': the physical, emotional and mental. When body, heart and mind are clear, then Spirit can flow through us. My teaching provides the tools for catharsis. Before I even begin to get spiritual, I teach you the tools of the trade to get you **onto your feet and moving**, to encourage you to **express yourself** and to guide you **into the gap in your mind**.

Over the next few chapters, I will show you how to do this.

● ●

How Empty Is Your Vessel?

Sit upright, close your eyes, relax your body and get in touch with your breath.

Spend a few minutes just watching your breath, watching the sensations in your body, watching your thoughts come and go.

Now see yourself as an empty vessel, like a 'hollow bamboo' – there is nothing inside, just emptiness. Be in this awareness for as long as you can.

It may be difficult for you to get a sense of this emptiness, you may be aware of your heaviness, tensions and discomfort. This is OK, just keep trying this for a few minutes now and then ... it will get easier. If you can experience the emptiness quite easily, then stay with it for as long as possible. After some time you may get a sense of being filled with a divine energy – enjoy it!

● ●

Chapter 8

Get Moving!

*As a warrior, just like any other animal, you have to be
able to run away from danger, if only from the danger of
your own madness.*

BAREFOOT DOCTOR

Your Body Is a Mirror

The state of your body is a mirror of the state of your being. Your body is a
holographic map of how you feel, think and move through life. Every feeling
that is ignored gets lodged in the body as tension. Every emotion that
remains unresolved gets locked in the body as pain. Every repetitive,
self-defeating, limiting thought gets recorded in the body as weakness.

This is how energy gets stuck in the body. Feelings, emotions and thoughts
are all forms of energy and when we hold on to them, they get stuck. Over
time, especially if we fill our bodies with junk food and we keep our bodies
inactive, this stuck energy stagnates and pollutes. When our life force does
not flow, we start to become lifeless, low in energy. Eventually we become
physically ill and psychologically out of balance. When energy does not
flow freely, we remain limited and small. A stuck body mirrors a stuck life.

In order to get stuck energy moving, we need to move! In our urban world, we are 'glued' to the TV, 'strapped' to our chairs, 'tied' to our desks, 'slouched' on our sofas and 'tucked up' in our beds ... movement does not appear to be a part of the modern equation! Yet our bodies are designed to walk, run, jump, bend, twist, sway and flow. When we move, the lubricating fluid between our joints gets stimulated and so we are well oiled, able to move freely without stiffness and pain. When we move, our bones get stronger because the application of pressure stimulates the production of minerals that 'bind' the bone. When we move, our muscles act like pumps, causing our blood to course through our veins and our lymph to circulate. Our blood carries vital nutrients as well as oxygen to all the cells, whilst the lymph drains away excess fluids, filters out toxins and produces antibodies to fight disease.

When we move, our internal organs and glands get massaged, stimulating them into action and releasing stuck energy. The liver, the lungs, the heart, the kidneys, the stomach and the bowels, all these benefit from regular movement. The cardiovascular system – heart, lungs and associated arteries and veins – is particularly important because it deals with the intake of that crucial life-giving force, oxygen. Oxygen contains high levels of *prana/chi* and so the more we can take in, the more alive and vibrant we become.

Regular movement that stimulates the cardiovascular system increases our capacity to take in oxygen. This is called fitness. The fitter we are, the more we can take in life! In other words, the more we can cope with without getting out of balance. My research in the 1980s led me to exactly this conclusion: the higher the fitness level, the more the capacity to deal with stress. Stress causes the release of hormones that basically pump up the body in preparation for thumping someone or running like hell! Your heart starts pounding, your face goes white as the blood drains away from your face, your muscles tense, your mouth goes dry, you start panting as your breathing rate increases, your teeth clench and your hands form into fists, you get a burst of energy as your adrenaline rises ... do you know the feeling?

This primitive but highly effective response to danger is fantastic if you live in the wild, fending off the barbarian beasts and tearing off your mate's knickers with your teeth. But if you live in the urban jungle where reaching for a morning croissant is about as far as you'll move and dealing with the onslaught of phone calls is about as physical as you'll get, then quite frankly you're in trouble. Every time you get stressed, this 'fight or flight' mechanism is activated. But with nowhere for you to go, the hormones go nowhere too. Just like your endless thoughts, worries and ruminations, they get stuck. Just like a needle stuck in the groove of a record, eventually the groove wears out. Your body, too, with constant repetition of the stress response, will wear out.

A stronger cardiovascular system, however, means that this stress response is not as intense and does not last as long. It is a little like putting pressure on a piece of elastic: the stronger the elastic, the more likely it is to retain its elasticity and spring back into shape. It is the same with being fit: the fitter you are, the more likely your physiological system stays in tip-top condition!

Your body is a hologram of who you are. Every part of your body mirrors a part of yourself. Just as the heart and lungs take in life-giving oxygen, so the cardiovascular system reflects how we cope with the demands of life. Not only can we see this in a more robust physiological functioning, but also in the ability to deal with stress. When the cardiovascular system is in poor condition, the lungs and heart are weak and so do we, too, collapse in the face of challenge. In this state, we perceive life's tasks as obstacles: in other words, we feel more stressed. Cardiovascular disease is a sign of closing off from life, there is a build up of fatty 'plaque' as life becomes all too much until finally the old motor packs up. Conversely, when the cardiovascular system is in tip-top condition, the heart and lungs are more powerful, pumping more oxygen, more blood, more vitality with less effort. We are literally more 'open' and so we take life's ups and downs in our stride: in other words, we are less 'stressed'.

The body's organs act like processors. Not only do they deal with chemical processes, but they also indicate how we process life. For example, the stomach is the seat of digestion. Not only does it release a cocktail of acid and enzymes to break down food into an absorbable condition, but it also shows us how we digest, assimilate, accept and make sense of life. If we do not like what we experience, we cannot 'take it', we cannot 'stomach it': our digestion literally gets impaired. Indigestion, ulcers, bloatedness and food allergies, all these are signs of a deep level of non-acceptance of what life has to offer.

Another good example is the intestinal system. Here we find the organs of elimination. It is the body's way of getting rid of anything indigestible or unsavoury. It is like dumping the garbage out every day in order to keep the house clean. This is our process of letting go, of releasing, of allowing the 'shitty' parts of life to pass through us. When we hold on to the experiences we label 'bad', when we are 'unable to let our shit go', then we become uptight, 'tight-assed', 'anal'. Eventually this negativity becomes toxic, poisoning our bodies, our emotions and our minds. Constipation, diarrhoea, intestinal gas, irritable bowel syndrome, diverticulosis, and haemorrhoids, all these are signs of an inability to let go.

Movement gently stimulates each bodily system so that it functions optimally. By releasing stuck energy, our whole body-mind system is enhanced, giving us physiological and psychological well-being. Since every level of being is interlinked, when we get things moving on a purely physical level then things start to shift on the other levels too.

I first learnt this when I started running as a regular form of exercise in my mid-twenties. Having been a couch potato for most of my life, I was sluggish and stodgy. Not only did I need to lose weight, but I also needed to lighten up my attitude to life. It was as if I carried the burdens of the world on my shoulders (and hips!). I saw life through grey-tinted glasses; I was withdrawn, miserable and grouchy. Little did I know that getting my body to shift gears would put a smile on my face! This 'feel good' factor was something I later subjected to rigorous scientific research during my post-graduate years at university. After examining hundreds of people who regularly did some kind of aerobic exercise, I concluded that physical exercise not only improves your physiological health but also balances your emotions, boosts your mood and lifts your spirit. In confirmation of my findings, other researchers in the US had started using aerobic exercise as a treatment for anxiety and depression.

When I looked more closely into the 'exercise high' phenomenon, I saw parallels with the heightened perception and mental acuity associated with peak experiences. Not only was there an increased blood flow and therefore oxygen supply to the brain, but there was also a sense of expanded consciousness where 'the flow' just happened. Not only was there a synchronization of brain wave patterns, but there was also a balancing of the analytical and creative sides of the mind so that internal chatter was transcended. Not only was there an increased production of endorphins – mood-enhancing hormones similar in effect to opiates – by the body's endocrine system, but there were also feelings of intense joy, bliss, peace, exhilaration and freedom.

These descriptions are reminiscent of the ecstatic, transcendent, mystical states found within spiritual disciplines. Certainly, for me, long-distance running has been a tool for meditation. When I run, the rhythm of my body is a mantra. The 'in and out' of my breath, the steady beat of my heart, the certainty of one foot following the other, the gentle swing of my arms, all these take me deeper into myself. When I run, time stands still and the world becomes one: I am no longer running, for there is no 'I' to do the running. When I run, I am in a state of beingness: I am in the flow, totally in the Now.

Telling Your Story

How your body moves mirrors how you move through life. Just watch yourself for a few moments, maybe as you walk across the room: do you drag yourself across, do you shuffle, limp, lope or leap? Do you feel heavy as if your body is a burden, do you feel awkward and clumsy, do you feel stiff? Or do you glide across the room, like a knife cutting through butter? Does your body feel light and graceful? Do you slide, slither and shimmy? How you stand, sit, walk and run, how you twist, bend and squat ... all these show how you carry yourself in the world: your attitudes, styles of behaviour, your interaction or relationship with life. This is your **body expression** ... and since your body is the vehicle of your soul, it is also your soul's expression. As Martha Graham, that great dance teacher, once said: 'The body never lies.'

Movement has been used as a healing practice and spiritual discipline for thousands of years. In the East, especially, there are numerous systems in which movement is used to develop body-mind unity and well-being, to increase self-awareness and to cultivate an expanded state of consciousness. In each tradition, the style of movement reflects the underlying philosophy and approach to life. For example, in Hatha yoga, the emphasis is on the rigorous application of self-discipline as the route to freedom. Hence the movements are very precise and orderly with the emphasis on staying in the position and just watching the body's tensions, emotions and thoughts as they play themselves out. It is very similar to the attitude of 'mindful meditation' in Buddhist traditions. In yoga, you are also encouraged to go beyond self-perceived limits within the mind-body and this of course then radiates out to spiritual development too.

T'ai chi, on the other hand, emphasizes free flowing movement with gentle rhythmic patterns. Based on the Taoist philosophy, this graceful martial art emphasizes the power of softness and the strength of yielding rather than opposing. Whilst aesthetically quite ethereal, there is nothing ephemeral about this: the core of t'ai chi teaches centredness in the body and groundedness in the feet. Other martial arts, too, are based on the development of inner strength through movement in harmony with natural forces. From the Japanese aikido to the Chinese wing chun to the Brazilian capoiera, each one of these different forms of movement cultivates a certain approach to life, a certain way of being. And yet they are all very similar as they all are based on a holistic approach to life.

Here in the West, there has been a much poorer tradition of movement as a path to self-development. With the patriarchal denial of the body there has come a neglect of the role of movement in holistic awareness. Whereas many of the movements and positions in Eastern disciplines are based on observations of animal poses and cycles of Nature – such as the dog pose in yoga, the crane in t'ai chi and the tree pose in chi kung – Western moves tend to be based on logical and numerical sequences that are aesthetically pleasing for their own sake. For example, both ballet and gymnastics are based on highly formalized routines. The body's natural rhythms are over-ridden and the emphasis is placed on the achievement of geometric and mathematical precision. This 'mind over matter' attitude appeals to the rational thinking mind; movement is forced, constricted. No wonder, then, that ballet dancers and gymnasts are so highly strung and that there is such a high incidence of injuries.

By contrast, in other parts of the East, where movement has been developed into an art form, its purpose has been to inspire the breadth of human emotions, to open the heart and expand the mind. From the delicate eroticism of a Japanese geisha's dance to the seductive charms of an Egyptian belly dancer, each one of these tells a story that is a part of the rich wealth of human experience.

It seems that how we move our bodies is a reflection of the cultural zeitgeist. In the West, with the rise of patriarchy, there has been a decreasing appreciation of the healing nature of movement. Instead,

97

male-dominated sports have taken over, where achievement, competition and sheer brute force have been the key elements. Women, especially, have been restricted to the kitchen and bedroom whilst physical freedom of expression has taken a back seat. Not until the exercise boom of the 1980s has physical movement played an important role in women's lives. The advent of the aerobics craze, popularized by Jane Fonda, has done much to empower women this century. By simply getting them back in touch with their bodies, this fad, which spread like wildfire across urban society, has emancipated women from stereotypes left over from the Victorian age such as the 'damsel in distress' and the 'wilting violet'. The archetypes of Athena, the Warrior Goddess, and Artemis, the Maiden Huntress, are alive and kicking in the gym of today! Women are now more physically and emotionally strong, more independent, more self-sufficient and more in charge of their lives than ever before!

I, too, found empowerment in the world of aerobics. As my physical strength increased so did my self-esteem, as my body shaped up so did the sharpness of my mind, and as my stamina improved so did my ability to be in control of my life. But, over time, I realized that the repetitive over-structured moves eventually led to burn out: not only physically but also emotionally and mentally. I was not listening to my body's innate wisdom and I was certainly not developing my spiritual self! I eventually realized that this type of exercise routine only develops strength of character, which is great up to certain point, but ultimately does not allow full exploration of the self and eventually leads to repression. Have you ever watched people in gyms? Or are you one of them? How do you feel when you watch (or do) those high-power kicks, the huff and puff of repetitive movements? Body builders, in particular, are obsessed with external results – a bigger, better, harder body is their aim! Yes, being pumped up gives them a boost – but at what price? Their will power is phenomenal but so are their psychological defences! An over-emphasis on muscular development leads to muscular armouring of the body-mind – rigid muscles are a sign of emotional stuckness!

Over the past few years, Eastern forms of movement have enjoyed a rising popularity, reflecting a more wholesome attitude to well-being. However, these too need to be approached with awareness. Yoga, wing chun and capoeira may all work with subtle energy, they may all enhance your *chi*, they may all develop spiritual awareness, but I still see a lot of people who get stuck in the outer form. The Western mind just loves structure and routine, it loves things to do. And so we can get attached to doing and feel good about ourselves, but this is just another ego thing! Nothing less than total awareness will do in such disciplines: it is only by bringing total awareness into the action that you get in touch with the subtle energy that guides the movement. Unfortunately, this is not something that comes easily to the Western mind or body so used to following orders and routines.

The Western mind does not need more discipline, more things to do, more things to learn and know... it just needs to let go, to be here now! The Western body does not need more structure and routine to follow ... it just needs to unwind, relax, loosen up, shake itself up! I have found that the less structured the movement, the more spontaneous, the more free and chaotic, then the greater the healing. In my teaching I use a variety of physical techniques to get energy moving. Whilst there is a basic structure to all of these, the crucial point is to follow your own natural energy cycle, your own natural rhythm. In this way, you access deeper and deeper levels of energy until you are in touch with the quantum body. It is here at this edge that you bring your awareness and it is here that there is expansion and healing.

By exploring the edge within each body part, from the tips of your toes to the top of your head, you begin to tell your story. As you move through layers of energy with your awareness, you will encounter blocks, knots of tension and discomfort, resistance. This is where energy has become stuck, this is where your history has been imprinted, woven into the fabric of your being. By bringing awareness here, you start to unravel these locked memories and so energy is released. This is the edge where movement happens, where your story starts to unfold. If you follow this movement, if you explore this edge, there is an expansion of energy. This is where you grow, where you move beyond your personal story, beyond the limitations of time and space, to encompass something greater, something infinite and eternal. As you weave in and out of this edge, exploring your boundaries, testing the possibilities, you create a unique dance. Every part of the body has a story to tell, every part of us is a part of the greater whole: the body is a hologram of life.

The Story of the Body

Feet are our foundation, our connection with the Earth beneath us, our grounding, our contact with reality. They give us our sense of balance, our sense of security and safety, our ability to 'hold our ground' and 'land on our feet' amidst the ever-changing circumstances of life. If our weight is unevenly distributed on our feet, then we are less likely to remain centred.

Feet also give us the ability to 'step out' into the world, to have a sense of direction and purpose, to 'move forwards'. If we tend to walk on our toes, then we are flitting through life without being totally present. If we are heavy-footed, digging into our heels, then we may be reluctant to move forwards.

Should we need to, we can also move backwards and sideways, thanks to our knees! Knees allow us to move in all directions, bringing flexibility and change into our lives. Knees give us a sense of ease as we weave in and out of situations, a sense of humility as we bow down to the higher path that life has carved out for us. Here is the crossroads where energy starts to flow upwards and the dance of inner and outer begins. Here is where inner conflict – 'Which path should I take?', 'What direction should I follow?' – becomes manifest as knee pain. When we are 'stuck in a rut', 'unable to take the right turn', knees become stiff. When we are too upstanding and take ourselves too seriously, we do not allow ourselves to bend with the flow of life and so we lose our spontaneity and playfulness.

As energy flows upwards through our legs, we experience the quality of our roots. Our legs are the position we take in life, our 'stance', our attitude to challenge. If our legs are weak, we topple over easily in the face of opposition, we 'don't have a leg to stand on'. Conversely, if our legs are tight and muscle-bound, we don't allow ourselves to budge an inch or give way to what life offers us. If our legs are heavy and clumsy, then we feel weighed down, unable to move lightly on our path. Legs indicate how we let energy flow upward to the spine: any blockages here will inhibit life-force from rising.

The spine is our support system, the centre around which everything else is kept together. If the spine is strong and stable yet flexible and yielding, then we can hold ourselves up whilst being able to flow with the tide of life – like a tree that sways in the wind, we survive the winds of change. But if our spine tends to collapse under pressure, if it bows down in submission at the slightest provocation, then we too are defeated. On the other hand, an overly rigid spine is a sign of inflexibility, of being too upright and brittle.

The pelvic area – which includes the hips, buttocks, lower belly and lower back – is a crucial point between the lower and upper parts of the body. If we hold ourselves in, with buttocks clenched, belly tucked in and pelvis locked, then we freeze the powerful energies, which would otherwise surge through us. If we cannot acknowledge our sexuality, if we are disgusted by our animal nature, then we push down our lower or base emotions. A frozen pelvis, one that feels tight and cannot move freely in all directions, is a sure sign that we are afraid of losing control, of giving in to our darker side.

When the pelvis is loose and relaxed and the belly soft and rounded, then energy continues to flow upwards into the chest cavity. This is where the different energies that flow through the body meet and mix. This is where we integrate all our feelings, emotions and thoughts and where we start to deal with them. Just as the heart and lungs are involved in the interchange of gaseous molecules, so it is here that the inner and outer worlds interact: it is here in the chest that we either open or close ourselves to the world. A sunken and narrow chest shows how we contract away from life, how we are weak, unable to cope with the world, unable to expand ourselves and extend outwards, unable to give. At the other extreme, an over-expanded chest is one that is 'pumped up' and shows how we are 'overblown' with our own self-importance, how we 'put on a front' in order to hide our vulnerability, how we are unable to take in any more of the world, unable to receive.

Moving on further up, the shoulders, arms and hands are our means of expression, for indeed these parts of the body speak volumes. Our shoulders reflect our attitude to responsibility, how we 'shoulder life'. If they are bowed and overly rounded, it is as if we are carrying the weight of the world, life is heavy, a burden. If they are hunched forwards so that the chest sinks in too, then we are creating a self-protective device, we are afraid of being hurt. If our shoulders are hunched up, it is as if we are in shock and we approach life with fear and tension. And if our shoulders are overly square, then we face life 'square on' with an air of machismo, we want the world to see our strength.

Our arms and hands are how we reach out and touch, hold, grasp, squeeze, hit, make, take and give. Over-developed arms are clumsy and awkward, showing an insensitivity and a reliance on brute strength or force to get things done. Under-developed arms, on the other hand, show a weakness and an inability to take a hold on life, a lack of initiative. Very thin, tight arms are wiry, grasping, clawing and clutching and show an agility in reaching out but an inability to hold on.

And finally, at the very top is our neck and head. This is how we face the world, how we look upon our environment. If our head is jutting forwards, then we tend to use our rational thinking self to lead the way. If our head is held up high, then we are proud and perhaps a little arrogant as we survey the world beneath us, but if our head droops down then we are unable to face reality, perhaps we are ashamed of ourselves. A stiff neck indicates an inability to see different points of view, a thick neck shows a bullish attitude, and a very thin neck shows a delicate and perhaps slightly anxious attitude … and so on and so on.

As you can see, the body has many tales to tell – it is all a matter of listening.

● ●

Try listening to your own story. You can do this exercise with or without music, but if you are using music, keep it very ambient.

Telling Your Story

Stand normally, close your eyes and take a few deep breaths. When you feel reasonably relaxed, bring your awareness down to your feet. Get a sense of how the weight of your body is balanced over your feet – is it even, over the heels, on the balls of your feet? Explore how it feels to change this balance: keep breathing deeply and regularly and allow the rest of your body to be loose and relaxed – see how changing the position of your feet affects the rest of the body. Now step forwards slowly with your full attention still in the feet – do you step lightly or heavily? Explore with your feet – slow steps, fast steps, on the toes, on the heels – how do you step out in the world?

Now draw the breath up into your knees and bring your total awareness here. Start to create movement with the knees, the rest of the body loose and relaxed. It is as if you have eyeballs in the knee joints and you are exploring the space around you. See how you move, forwards, backwards, sideways, up and down ... what are the sensations in your knees? Are they stiff and rigid? Is there pain and resistance? Or do they feel well oiled, light and bouncy?

Now bring your awareness into your thighs. See how your whole legs move. Do you move with stealth and strength or are your legs shaky and unsure? How do you carry yourself forwards?

Now draw the breath upwards through your spine. Become aware of each vertebra, the sensations as you stretch and bend. Become aware of any places in the spine that feel stiff – how does this affect the rest of your body? How do you carry yourself – are you upright and unyielding or do you bend and give way?

And your hips – do they feel smooth, can you create circles or are your movements jerky and awkward, do they feel stiff? Is it pleasurable or embarrassing to move your hips and pelvis?

Now breathe into your chest cavity. Is there any freedom of movement here, do you feel expansive? Or do you feel caged in, held back somehow?

And the shoulders – is there much pain and stiffness here, do they feel heavy and tight?

Let your breath travel down your arms and into your hands, stretching and extending outwards. What are your hands doing? Are they clutching, clenching? Or are they soft and gentle?

Now check out your neck. Let your head drop forwards and let it roll gently side to side. Check out your jaw – is it clenched tight or nice and loose? What about the rest of your face? You'll be amazed at the amount of tension held here!

Finally, draw your breath up to the crown of the head ... and gently allow yourself to come to a standstill.

● ●

● ●

Things to Do (or Be) Every Day

- WALK whenever you can ...or take the dog for a walk!
- Jog/run – get a good pair of trainers and build up slowly. Do it in the park if you can.
- Go to the gym – any form of movement is better than none! Just beware you don't get stuck on trying to be the fastest/strongest/leanest/wearing the best outfit!
- Take up something more holistic – t'ai chi, yoga, chi kung, aikido, wing chun, capoiera, any other martial art that grabs your fancy or any other mind-body system with a fancy name!

- DANCE – try belly dancing, salsa, trance-dance, 5Rhythms, Biodanza. Go to a club, go to a party, dance at home – dance when you're happy, dance when you're sad, dance when you're angry – just put on some music and MOVE!
- BE FLEXIBLE – stretch once in a while, especially if you sit at a desk all day long. Get up and reach your arms to the ceiling, bend forwards and let your upper body hang, rotate your shoulders, let your head roll – just loosen up!
- BE ACTIVE – do anything, JUST GET MOVING!

Chapter 9

Express Yourself!

> *We're all scared. We're all angry. We're all sad. That's a given. The question is, what are we going to do about it?*

GABRIELLE ROTH

Energy in Motion

Emotion is **energy in motion**. When this energy is not moving, then it is a stuck emotion. When we repress, suppress, ignore and deny our feelings, then we block the natural flow of energy. Feelings are experienced in the body – how else would we feel something? When we are in touch with our feelings, we are aware of energy moving and so we feel alive ... remember, life-force/*prana*/*chi* is awareness in motion. But when we are out of touch with our feelings, we are also cut off from our bodies, and so we are not aware of energy moving. When we are out of touch with our feelings, life-force/*prana*/*chi* is stagnant and so we feel lifeless.

This stuck energy has nowhere to go, it remains trapped inside the body. And like any living thing that is trapped, it will start to create havoc. A feeling that is not totally felt, that is not given the space to exist, that is not allowed to just 'be', will turn into resentment, it will become a grudge. An emotion that is not given freedom of expression, that is not acknowledged, that is not honoured, eventually becomes distorted. What starts off as simply a feeling, eventually becomes a monster that is out of control. What starts off as simply energy moving, becomes emotional instability and eventually physical illness.

The most common example of energy in motion is anger. Try to imagine what it feels like to be angry. Imagine, just for a moment, an incident or situation that has made you angry: what does it feel like in your body? Anger, when you are aware of it, is very tangible: your body starts to feel hot in some places, your muscles tighten, your jaw clenches ... there is a definite sensation of a powerful energy moving through you. However, mostly, we lose our awareness when anger takes us over and so we lose touch with our body and jump into our head with thoughts such as 'You bastard, it's your fault!', 'I hate you, how could you do that to me?' and 'You are totally wrong, I don't want to talk to you anymore!'. Equally often, we are so cut off from our feelings, that we are not even aware that we are angry in the first place and so anger remains unexpressed: someone close to us may ask, 'What's wrong with you?' and our reply is 'Oh, nothing!'

Unexpressed anger most often is turned inwards to become self-blame and guilt and eventually depression. Depression is simply stuck anger. What started off as a simple need to express an uncomfortable feeling, becomes a malignant entity that eats away at us, making us feel low. Over an extended period of time, this may manifest as an illness such as cancer or irritable bowel syndrome. Sometimes, rather than being turned inwards, anger is turned outwards in an outburst of destructive rage. This is not only harmful to the person who is being 'dumped' on but also to the person who is doing the 'dumping'. Rage increases stress levels, it over-stimulates the adrenal glands, taxes the liver and strains the heart. When rage is really out of control, the build up of energy is so great that it can no longer be contained and so it explodes into physical violence in order to disperse the charge. The legacy of the mishandling of anger is clear to see in the high incidence of domestic violence, street crime and general vandalism that are becoming features of the modern urban world. At the extreme end of the scale, we see human rights violations, genocide and warfare.

Actually, anger is usually a mask for an underlying feeling of fear. Anger is a natural response to feeling threatened in some way, it shows us where we are vulnerable. When we do not acknowledge this vulnerability, we allow our fear to create a block. Unacknowledged fear just builds up more and more blocks, resistances, walls of armouring to protect us from the flood of feelings that would overwhelm us if we let our guard down. Fear is a holding on, an inability to let go and feel the pain of having been hurt, an inability to feel the pain of loss, whether this be the loss of a loved one, the loss of a job or the loss of our innocence. When we cannot let go, we are frozen and our tears are like ice, unable to flow. If we cannot express sadness, then neither can we experience joy, for our heart remains closed. Anger is simply a barrier that we put up to protect ourselves from pain.

Emotions are simply energy: what makes the difference between a 'heavy' emotion, like anger, and a 'light' emotion, like joy, is the frequency of vibration. A heavy emotion is slower, in other words, more dense, and a lighter emotion is faster, in other words, less dense. The more dense an emotion, the more tangible it is, that is, the easier it is to get in touch with it, and vice versa. For example, anger is actually easier to access than joy.

Anyone who is unable to contact their anger and yet claims to be happy is actually living a lie. True happiness, true joyfulness can only be accessed when anger has been moved out of the way. Joy comes from an open heart, one that has plumbed the depths of despair as well as the heights of ecstasy. When joy is given room for expression, then love is the flower that blooms. Love is not sympathy or pity. Love is not need or desire. Love is the fragrance of an open heart. And love can only grow when anger, fear, resentment and guilt have been moved out of the way.

Today's urban world allows little opportunity for the free expression of emotions. Anger is the most denied, misunderstood and yet widespread emotion that we experience as modern people. Because anger is the most accessible emotion, because it lies at the surface, it is the first emotion that needs expression before being able to contact the less tangible ones. Without the expression of anger, there is ultimately no love. I see a lot of 'spiritual avoidance' when it comes to anger. It is a common ego trap to believe that to be spiritual means not getting angry. Not only is this misconception encouraged in New Age circles but it is also espoused in Eastern teachings such as Buddhism. It is not so much a fault of the teachings, but rather a common misunderstanding or pitfall along the path of spiritual development.

In the case of New Age teachings, the emphasis is usually on changing the negative thought of anger to a positive one of forgiveness. Unfortunately, this does not actually deal with truly feeling the anger, it does not get the energy moving, and so it just moves further underground – this is repression. In the case of Buddhist teachings, the attitude is to 'just sit and watch' the anger until it passes. This is great if you are quite developed spiritually, if you can really be with total awareness of the anger: in other words, if you can stay fully in the body and watch the energy moving. Yes, the anger will pass, it will transform – but most of us are not at this stage and all that happens is more repression. In particular, such an attitude is neither helpful or relevant to the modern-day stressed-out person.

When we block the free expression of our emotions, we create layer upon layer of stuckness. How can we be truly spiritual if we are full of repression? How can there be room for Spirit to flow through us if we are 'full of crap'? I know this one because for years I lived in denial of my anger. I stuffed my anger so far down that I cut myself off from being truly alive. I was so scared of pain that I missed out on experiencing the totality of life. I was so busy trying to be 'nice' that I lived life on the surface, I was lukewarm, passionless, lacking in real depth. Actually, I was depressed because my anger was stuck and the result was that my body was severely constipated. It was only after much prodding, pushing, shoving and shaking – physically, emotionally and mentally – that things started to shift. It was only after I, almost literally, had the stuffing knocked out of me that I could allow myself to get real and get angry. It was only then that energy got moving and I started to enjoy life.

What is needed for most of us is a deep cleansing, a catharsis. It is a little like having a bath or a shower: our stuck emotions need to be washed away. What has become dirty, murky, muddy, heavy, needs to be made clean, clear, fresh and light. What has been laden down needs to be en-lightened. Emotions need to keep moving, feelings need to keep flowing. When water flows, it stays fresh and vibrant, life-affirming. But when water becomes stagnant, it plain and simply stinks! Emotions are just like water:

when we give them permission to move through us, we stay healthy, but when we dam them up, we suffer.

If we allow an emotion room for expression, it will quite quickly change its vibration to a higher frequency. Anger given full expression will become fear will become hurt will become sadness will become joy will become love. It is only when we put a stop on an emotion that it stays stuck. The natural state of emotions is fluidity, changeability, liquidity. When emotions are allowed to flow, to follow their own natural course, then they will naturally transform. And so we are cleansed, refreshed, replenished ... we are born anew.

Let It Out!

Movement is the nature of our emotional state. Habitually stuck emotions become habitual blocks in the physical body. If our feelings are not flowing then neither are our bodies. I see this time and time again in my teaching practice. I see locked jaws, stiff necks, crossed arms, locked pelvises, rigid knees ... and these are people who have come to move, to dance! How can you move freely, how can you dance joyfully if all your energy is spent holding onto or stuffing down feelings? You need to release this energy. Before you can enjoy the dance, you need to get in touch with the feelings in your body. Dance is an expression of the self, so before we dance, I use movement to facilitate emotional expression. I use the breath to get in touch with the inner body, to bring awareness to what is hidden, so that energy can get moving.

In my workshops, I provide a safe space to express those parts of yourself that are usually hidden. Here you can unburden yourself of those parts that you have labelled 'unacceptable', 'dark' or 'bad'. Here you can play out your sub-personalities, you can give yourself permission to explore your many selves. You can shout your anger, stomp your rage, scream your fear, cry your anguish, wail your grief and laugh yourself silly. Here it is OK to feel lust, envy, greed, vanity and confusion. You can be as wild as an animal and as innocent as a child. Here it is OK to be as crazy as you like!

● ●

Here are some of my favourite tools to help you express yourself.

This first exercise involves 'chaotic breathing', which helps to break up the rigid thinking patterns of the rational brain as well as activating primal emotions. It is a powerful but perfectly safe process, which creates chaos so as to jolt you out of your stuckness and wake you up.

Make sure you are in private space with nothing to bump into, perhaps have some cushions handy. If you can, put some music on, preferably something with a chaotic rhythm, either tribal or rock; you can also do this without music but it helps a little. And blow your nose before you start!

Catharsis

Stand with your feet hip-width apart so you have a strong base, soften your knees and keep the rest of the body relaxed and close your eyes.

Start breathing in and out of the nose rapidly, allowing the breath to go deep into your chest – make sure the shoulders, arms and neck stay relaxed.

Allow the breath to be chaotic – NOT a steady rhythm! Some breaths are short, others are long, some slow, some fast ... KEEP CHANGING THE RHYTHM! Be as chaotic as you can. As the intensity builds up, you will find that your whole body starts to move too. You can help the chaotic breathing by using your arms like bellows but remember to keep relaxed and keep the knees soft and bouncy.

Keep going for at least 5 minutes, preferably 10. You may feel as if you are 'losing your mind' ... that's great, welcome the feeling!

When the intensity has built up quite high, just let go! Allow yourself to go crazy – scream, shout, cry, laugh, let the sounds come out. Use physical movements to express your emotions – punch a cushion, roll around the floor, shake – keep moving! If this is not possible because of neighbours, then keep the sounds quiet but allow the energy to be expressed through your movements.

Keep going for about 10 minutes or until you feel empty.

Lie down in silence ... be still.

Go Crazy!

Sit on the floor with your eyes closed, relax your facial muscles, especially the jaw.

Start letting sounds come out of your mouth, gibberish like a child – be playful.

Allow this to build up so that you involve the body by moving, rocking, shaking your arms, rolling your head, etc. – be like a crazy person, don't hold back!

Continue for about 10 minutes and then stop and sit still in silence for a few minutes.

(ADAPTED FROM OSHO'S *Dynamic Meditation*, and *Gibberish*)

● ●

● ●

Things to Do (or Be) Every Day

*   STOP DOING for a few minutes and LISTEN TO YOUR BEING ... check in with your FEELINGS by doing a quick 'body scan'. Close your eyes and check and let your awareness move around your body. Which areas are tense, tight, heavy, etc.? Just FEEL what is going on here – that's all!
*   LET IT OUT! If an intense emotion is just festering inside or waiting to burst out, then – if you have the luxury of privacy – GO A LITTLE CRAZY! Jump up and down on the bed, get a pillow and beat it, scream into the duvet, kick, shake, roll around ... just don't hurt yourself! Keep going until you feel lighter, clearer and freer.
*   If you're feeling particularly stuck or low – or if it's not appropriate to let it all out by screaming and jumping. Then take a pen and WRITE –

anything, everything, just let it free flow without censoring it – don't think, just write! Keep going until you feel lighter, clearer and freer.

- BE CHILDLIKE! Be playful, spontaneous, laugh, etc.

● ●

Chapter 10

Mind the Gap!

That's what you always forget, isn't it? I mean, you forget to pay attention to what's happening. And that's the same as not being here and now.

ALDOUS HUXLEY, *Island*

Thought Waves

The mind is like a radio receiver: it picks up whatever is being carried on the airwaves. Thoughts are mental energies that are carried across the airwaves and are picked up by the receiver. A 'heavy' thought, such as 'My life is miserable', is a denser energy than a 'light' thought, such as 'Today is wonderful'. By tuning into a particular frequency, your receiver will pick up the thought that matches it on an energetic level. A receiver that is tuned in to a narrow frequency band will pick up a smaller range of thought energies than one that has a wider band capacity. The more your mind expands, the wider the range of thoughts. The broadest band is when your mind has expanded into big mind. Here, your receiver can pick up cosmic or divine thoughts, such as 'All is Perfect', 'Miracles are acts of love' and 'I am All That Is' – this is Universal Mind or the Mind of God.

Unfortunately, today's lifestyle programmes our receiver to pick up a narrow range of frequencies. The hustle and bustle of daily life in the modern city, the stress and strain of urban life, the rushing around to get things done, the pushing and shoving to get there first, all this keeps our receiver tuned in to the frequency of survival, achievement, doing and having. This attracts thoughts such as 'I must fight my way to the top', 'I must get this/that/the other done on time' and 'I must have that pair of shoes or I'll die!'. It encourages thoughts of lack, inadequacy and incompleteness, such as 'I'm not good enough', 'There's never enough money to go round', 'I wish I could have everything I want' and 'One day all my dreams will come true and I'll be happy'. These are thoughts of limitation. This is small mind.

These kinds of thoughts are focused on the past and the future. Since the past is dead and the future is yet to be born, these snapshots of time are not alive. And if they are not alive then they must be stagnant, in other words, they are stuck moments of time. And this is exactly what these types of thoughts are – stuck! They go round and round in our heads, like an endless feedback loop. There is no solution: we cannot change the past for it has already happened, and we cannot absolutely know the future for it has not happened yet. And so we are trapped, bound by the limitations of time. When we remember the past, we are attached to memories, and when we fantasize about the future, we are attached to projections. These thoughts are stuck mental energy, mental junk that we are holding onto because our receiver has a limited band frequency.

The accumulation of mental junk creates a constant background noise of worry, anxiety and stress. We cannot totally relax because in the back of our minds are these niggling thoughts that keep telling us that things aren't quite right. We cannot be totally at ease because we are not yet satisfied; our lives are not yet totally fulfilled for we are not yet fully aware of our true nature.

What keeps us stuck is a lack of awareness. Lack of awareness means we are not fully present. Awareness brings us right into the present moment, the Now. Every moment is a 'Now', and so, by continually bringing our awareness into the present moment, the Now becomes eternal. This is where time expands, where time is freed from the bondage of past and future. Where there is expansion, there is movement; and so now mental energy becomes unstuck. Movement means letting go, so stuck thoughts can be released, they can be cleared. Letting go means simply watching. It does not mean getting rid of thoughts by pushing them away, denying or suppressing them. Neither does it mean replacing negative thoughts with positive thoughts. This is just 'spiritual band aid' and will only plaster over the negativity for a while until it bursts through again with even greater force. Thoughts are thoughts, whether positive or negative: the point is to transcend the thinking mind. Thinking is a **doing**, whereas letting go means letting **be**. It means giving all thoughts permission to exist, giving them some breathing room, some space to move. Letting be means the mind can relax a little, it can let go of its tight grip, it can loosen up, lighten up a little. Now the mind is more natural.

The nature of mind is movement ... thoughts come and go, they ebb and flow just like waves on an ocean. You cannot obliterate a thought but you can watch it. If you follow its course, you will see that it arises from nothingness, reaches a peak and then it recedes back into nothingness. A thought in its natural state is always moving. A thought is like the wind: if allowed the freedom to move, it just comes and goes, clearing away the clutter and bringing fresh energy. But if it is contained, if it is held onto, it will get stuffy, dust will gather and cobwebs will accumulate.

To watch our thoughts is to be **mindful**. This does not mean to have a mind full of thoughts. Being 'mindful' is the opposite of being 'mindless'. In other words, being mindful is being attentive, observant, watchful, aware: being mindless is being unaware. It is only in a state of awareness that there is movement; it is only in a state of awareness that we can watch thoughts come and go. And paradoxically, it is only in a state of mindfulness that we can discover the emptiness of mind. By watching thoughts arise and fall away, we eventually observe **the space between thoughts**. I call this **minding the gap**.

● ●

This is good to practise for a few minutes every day.

Mind the Gap

Sit upright comfortably, either cross-legged or on a straight-backed chair. Close your eyes and take a few deep breaths, letting your body relax.

Turn your attention to your mind, becoming aware of all the thoughts that are racing past. There is no need to do anything other than just WATCH how these thoughts are moving through your mind.

Now gently turn your attention to the GAP between thoughts. Yes, just as one thought ends and another begins there is a short pause – it may be only fractional, but as you keep bringing your attention here this gap will grow. You may find that you keep getting caught up in your thoughts again and losing your awareness – this is fine, just gently keep bringing your attention back to the gap.

● ●

Minding the gap requires alertness, or else you will trip and fall, your natural flow will be interrupted, all movement will stop, you will get stuck. If you mind the gap, if you bring your total awareness into the space between thoughts, you have entered the Now. Here you become aware of the stillness of eternity. In this timeless place, you experience the emptiness that lies behind the activity of the mind. This is the edge between form and formless, the place of expansion. Now you have moved beyond small mind, you transcend the limitations of thinking and you expand into Big Mind.

This is meditation. This is where you realize your true nature, where you touch the 'real I'. **This is the place of wisdom, where your mind is one with the Mind of God.**

Meditation Is Being

Meditation is a state of **being**. It is rather misleading that we say 'to meditate': it implies that we are **doing** something, but actually it is the complete opposite. As Osho says: 'You cannot do meditation, you can only be in meditation. It is not a question of being. It is not an act but a state.' (OSHO, *Autobiography of a Spiritually Incorrect Mystic*)

Again, this misunderstanding, this confusion, is something that I frequently encounter in my teaching practice. When I mention the word 'meditation', I often get the response, 'Oh, what kind of meditation?'. My answer is, there is only one kind of meditation — and that is the state of total awareness, of absolute mindfulness. It is the same story as with understanding the meaning of Tantra and it is the same story as with understanding the spiritual path.

We must take care not to confuse the knowledge of the form, the method, with the experience itself. The former is doing, the latter is being. The former is simply a tool, a technique. And there are many techniques of meditation: there is Transcendental Meditation, Vipassana, Anapana, Mettabhavna, Dzogchen, Zen, Nadabrahma, Golden Light Meditation, Mystic Rose Meditation … and so many more. In the ancient text, the *Vigyan Bhairav Tantra*, in which the Lord Shiva passed on his wisdom to help humanity, there are 112 methods outlined: each one brings you to the same place.

These are all tools to help you come to the place of meditation. Meditation is not a doing, rather it is an *un*doing. The rich variety of tools for meditation has been developed over the ages to help you undo the layers of 'false self' that you carry. These are ways to help you let go of this burden that weighs you down, that prevents your true self from shining through.

Another comment I frequently hear in response to meditation is, 'Oh, I can't meditate: it's too difficult.' How can meditation be difficult? It is the most natural state to be in. Being in meditation is being relaxed, loose, at ease. Being in meditation is being, awake, aware, alive. Meditation is 'passive alertness'. It is the state of small babies and animals. Have you watched a cat sitting in the sun apparently doing nothing yet totally attuned to the movements of a small bird close by? Have you gazed into the eyes of a tiny infant and got lost in the vibrancy of the moment? It is the most natural state in the world! Being in meditation is not sitting in lotus position performing complex chants or mental acrobatics. You can be in meditation anywhere, anytime. In fact, you can be in meditation everywhere, all the time. It is simply being present – totally. It is being in touch with reality, not living in some kind of half-awake fantasy world. It is very simple really!

What is difficult, though, is that in the process of waking up, in the process of becoming aware, you encounter your blocks, your resistance. In other words, as you expand into consciousness, you also become aware of your *un*consciousness. This is the threshold, the discomfort zone. It is a little like stepping into the bright sunlight after you have spent most of your life hiding in a dark cave. Initially, it feels uncomfortable, you feel exposed, vulnerable, you want to withdraw once more into the darkness. Slowly though, with practice, the light feels welcoming, you get a sense of freedom here, you can stretch a little, grow a little, spread your wings. In the light, you start to see clearly, you get a bigger picture of life. In the light, you start to open your eyes, there is so more much to explore than you had imagined ... it starts to feel good.

As you step more and more into the light of awareness, what is false in you starts to drop away, to dissolve. The critical, demanding, whining voice of the ego loses its impetus, the endless chatter of the many selves recedes into the background. All these are transcended as you experience the reality of who you really are. **Meditation is getting out of your head and into your heart** – into your centre. Meditation is standing in the centre of your being. When you stand in the centre, it is like the sun is shining directly above you. Here no shadow is cast and so you have a clear view all the way round, 360 degrees. Here, nothing is 'in the dark', nothing is hidden, nothing is unconscious.

When consciousness expands so that it is no longer trapped in your head, then it fills up your whole being, you become complete. Now mind and body are one. Now you are centred in your heart – and breath is the key that opens this centre.

● ●

Try this at any time.

Just Sit and Watch

Sit comfortably, either cross-legged or in a straight-backed chair. Close your eyes, take a few deep breaths and relax your body.

Just sit and DO NOTHING! WATCH how your body just sits there, watch how your breathing just happens, just watch how your mind is active.

Every time you catch yourself drifting off, getting caught up in your thoughts, bring your awareness back to the NOW – and just WATCH!

● ●

● ●

Things to Do (or Be) Every Day

- BE ATTENTIVE. WATCH THE GAP in everything you do – whether you are sitting, standing, walking, running, washing dishes, making love, or whatever.
- STOP and DO NOTHING!
- Become the SKY. Choose a day when the sky is clear and just watch it. Watch the clarity, the expansiveness, the stillness, the emptiness. Feel it. Become it!

● ●

Chapter 11

Breathe, Breathe, Breathe!

> *Breathing is the most important thing in life. Everything else can wait.*

BAREFOOT DOCTOR

Breath is the Key

Breath is the key to life. Breath keeps us alive. We may survive without food for lengthy periods of time, and even without water for some time, but without breath we die pretty rapidly. From the first inhalation we take at the moment of birth to the last exhalation we make at the point of death, breath carries us through the journey of life. Breath is movement. When breath flows through us, we are alive. When breath stops, we are dead. There are no two ways about it!

Breath is energy moving, it is life-force itself. Breath is *prana/chi*, it is our vital essence. When we breathe fully, we are full of vitality, full of life, full of energy. When our breathing is impaired in some way, we are devitalized, lifeless, lacking in energy. Breathing is the mechanism by which we convert energy into Matter. Every breath we take transforms prana into the 'stuff of life', the raw materials which keep our whole body-mind functioning. Every cell in our body needs this energy to create the biological processes that keep us alive. Every movement, action, decision and thought, whether conscious or unconscious, relies on this energy.

Oxygen is the physical manifestation of this energy. Oxygen is the catalyst that ignites the spark of life. It is oxygen that is extracted by the lungs from the air that we breathe and then transported by the blood to every single cell in the body. It is oxygen that powers the nervous system and feeds the brain. Many common ailments such as chronic fatigue, anxiety, headaches, general aches and pains, and asthma can be traced back to poor breathing habits, which limit the amount of oxygen we receive. Oxygen therapy has been used in some medical circles to treat a variety of illnesses, from eczema to herpes and from flu to AIDS. When the body is well-oxygenated, it has the energy to assimilate nutrients, eliminate toxins, repair damage and recharge the batteries. When we are well oxygenated, every fibre of our being vibrates with vitality. Oxygen sustains our bodies, rebalances our emotions and enhances our minds. When we are supercharged with oxygen, we feel vibrant, clear and light. An abundance of oxygen makes us high!

● ●

Try taking 20 deep inhalations and exhalations now and feel the difference!

● ●

Breathe Now!

Breath has the power to affect us deeply. How we think, feel, move and act are intimately connected with how we breathe. How we breathe is how we live. Wherever we are stuck in life, so is our breathing. When we hold onto our emotions and thoughts, we limit our breath. This holding on is reflected in our bodies. Every feeling we are frightened to acknowledge, every emotion we try to block out, every thought we obsess over, all these cause us to hold our breath for fear of letting go. And all these create a stuckness in our physical structure, which further limits our full breathing capacity. Body-mind therapies such as Reichian bodywork, Rolfing and Bioenergetics, call this process 'muscular armouring'. This means exactly what it says: every time we hold back from the full experience of our feelings, we create tension in certain muscles and eventually these muscles become habitually rigid. In other words, we create a physical suit of armour to protect ourselves from feeling the pain. We put up a guard to shut the world out and shut ourselves in.

This self-created prison may seem like a safe refuge from the harshness of the world outside but it only serves to limit us. By not experiencing life as it really is, we are simply keeping the pain locked in our bodies and harming ourselves in the long run. By blocking life out, we are numbing ourselves to the rich wealth of feelings, intuitions and insights that lie deep within us all. By limiting the full expression of the self, we also limit the power of our creativity and our sexuality and we curtail our capacity for ecstasy, love and joy. We cannot be whole if we do not fully breathe!

Over the years I have been teaching, I have never ceased to be amazed at the power of breath. I also never ceased to be amazed at the resistance many people have to breathing fully. People of all age groups and from all walks of life come to my workshops and classes to find freedom through movement, to dance and to enjoy themselves ... but they do not expect to breathe! Usually, before we start anything else, I ask everyone to bring their attention to their breath. Sometimes we simply do this by sitting still and concentrating on the chest rising and falling and other times we do this by standing and focusing on the various body parts. At this point, I already detect a lot of inner resistance and restlessness. Most people start to fidget and look uncomfortable. They start to frown and wonder why they have come to a movement/dance workshop when I am asking them to breathe instead! Once we have overcome this little hurdle, my focus throughout is still on the breath. I use a variety of breathing techniques, some gentle and some more powerful, to get energy moving. Breathing fully awakens repressed feelings, it releases suppressed energy. If you allow these feelings to bubble up to awareness, this stuck energy will move through your body and be released. **Here is the freedom you are looking for!**

Once in a while, someone comes along who is so busy shutting out what they have labelled 'pain' or 'discomfort' or 'bad' that they simply refuse to breathe. This person will just stand there, knees rigid, pelvis locked, arms folded across their chest and throat constricted. There is so much energy used up in pushing things down, shutting things out that this person can hardly move. When I ask why they are here, most often such a person tells me it's because they 'love to dance'. My answer is: 'how can you dance without feeling, and how can you feel without breathing?'

● ●

Try this now.

Breathe Now!

Sit upright, either cross-legged or in a straight-backed chair, close your eyes and relax your body.

Breathe gently and naturally through your nose, letting yourself settle into a steady rhythm. As you breathe in and out of your nose, just WATCH the breath come and go. Really bring your whole awareness to the sensations as your breath enters and leaves your nostrils. Continue for a few minutes.

Now bring your attention down to the centre of your chest, just WATCHING how the chest rises and falls as your breath comes and goes. Stay aware of all the sensations and feelings that arise here. Continue for a few minutes.

Now bring your attention down to your lower belly, just WATCHING how the belly rises and falls as the breath comes and goes. Again stay aware of the sensations and feelings here. Continue for a few minutes.

Finally, bring your awareness back to the breath entering and leaving your nostrils. Slowly open your eyes when you are ready.

● ●

What I see is a fear of being fully present. Breathing fully means embracing all of yourself. Resistance to breathing is simply the ego's attempt at self-preservation. Because your ego judges parts of your self to be bad, it tries to hide these unacceptable selves at all costs. The shame of exposing your vulnerability is too much for the ego to bear! But this safeguarding is ultimately at your own expense. Releasing shame, blame and guilt is a liberating experience. Without this, the ego will continue to construct more and more elaborate ways to defend itself. In the end, the true light of your own inner beauty and glory will not shine through.

The Power of Breath to Heal

Bringing awareness to the breath is a powerful tool for healing and transformation. Breath is like the wind: it clears away the debris, it uncovers layers of resistance until old wounds are revealed for healing. Just like a physical wound, an emotional wound cannot be healed unless it is aired. In both cases, a wound that is covered up, concealed or ignored, will fester and become toxic. Breath cleanses these old hurts by bringing them to awareness, by bringing them into the present moment. It is only in the Now that this stuck energy can move and be released.

Breath peels back the layers until the primary wound is revealed. This is the primal breath, the first breath you ever took. This first intake of air is a template for how you take in life. Because birth is our primary experience of life, because it is such a hugely epic 'life and death' struggle, the breathing patterns we develop at this time act like a blueprint for our approach to life.

Of course, each and every one of us undertakes the journey from the safety of the womb, suffering the contractions of the uterus, the expulsion down the birth canal and the squeeze through to the light at the end of the tunnel. And for each and every one of us, the journey through the life that follows is filled with pleasure and pain, highs and lows, hope and despair ... each of us struggles to be reborn in every moment. However, it is clear that modern birthing techniques have compounded a precarious, although otherwise natural, phenomenon. Constant foetal monitoring, adherence to timetables and premature intervention using surgical procedures ... all this interferes with the natural birth process. And once removed from the all-encompassing bliss-state of the womb, there is more hostility. The bright lights of the hospital room, the loud voices of the nursing staff, the rough handling in the name of sanitation, the harsh environment and stressful atmosphere ... all this serves to unnecessarily traumatize the super-sensitive newborn. It is a patriarchal view that birth is a medical emergency!

In particular, the premature cutting of the umbilical cord is pivotal in causing the first breath to be taken in complete distress. It is at this point that the transition between the mother's oxygen supply and the newborn's ability to use his or her own lungs is severely disrupted. What a welcome to the world! What usually follows adds insult to injury. Most often the poor little thing is suspended upside down and given a hard slap – wouldn't you scream too? And this is followed by an abrupt separation from the mother, insensitive handling, strict feeding routines ... all these serve to further alienate such a delicate creature.

It seems that the stress and alienation many of us experience in the modern world mirrors the stress and alienation of the medical approach to birth.

Such traumas create a contraction. To withdraw energetically from what is perceived to be dangerous and hostile is only natural. Of course, we cannot avoid all unpleasant experiences: life is full of ups and downs. However, when the trauma is deeply embedded in our primal cellular memory and if it is exacerbated by painful childhood experiences – as many of us have had – then the contraction becomes habitual. It is not so much that painful experiences are bad, rather that we have not been taught how to resolve them, how to move through them, how to breathe.

Since the publication in the late 1970s of Leboyer's classic book, *Birth Without Violence*, which beautifully describes the journey we all undertake at birth, there has been much evidence to support the notion that birth trauma affects us for life. From the detailed work of Leonard Orr and Sondra Ray on 'birth scripts' to the more recent discoveries by psychologists of the 'secret life of the unborn child', all agree that modern birthing techniques are basically barbaric! Since then, more humane birthing methods have been popularized, such as non-interventional home births and water births. Babies born in this way have been shown to have a higher IQ, to be more creative, more psychic, to be emotionally stable, happy and peaceful. Perhaps as more babies are born in this holistic way, our urban environment will also reflect this harmony.

Breath is one of the greatest healing forces that exists. The fact that most body-mind therapies as well as almost all spiritual disciplines see breath as the key to awareness and healing is a testament to this. Western body-mind therapies, based on Reich's seminal work on breath and 'body-armouring', along with the many variations of 'rebirthing' therapies have all developed from an understanding of the relationship between breathing patterns and life attitudes.

In the body-mind spiritual practices of the East too, 'right breathing' is a central issue. The aim is to open the body's energy channels so that breath may flow freely. In this way, health and wholeness are achieved. Many meditation techniques, such as Anapana and Vipassana, also involve breath awareness. Here, breath is the entry point into the present moment. And in the more esoteric disciplines, such as Pranayama and Tantric energy-work, breath is also the magic ingredient for expanding consciousness.

Making breath conscious is making life conscious. Whether I work with groups or with individuals, my focus is on **conscious connected breathing**. Whether your birth memory is activated or not, whether you remember a past-life or whether you imprint positive thoughts to replace negative ones is not so important. You simply need to breathe and experience energy moving. Focus on the body, on feeling energy moving through your body.

There are a variety of breathing techniques to facilitate the release of emotions, to break up the rigidity and control of the rational thinking mind and to expand consciousness into higher realms. You have already experimented with chaotic breathing for breaking up mental and emotional stuckness in a previous chapter (pages 114–16). Later you will meet a more specialized technique called the **Breath of Fire**. But the technique I use most often is circular breathing. Here, the inhale and the exhale are connected, the breath is one continuous flow, creating a 'circle of breath'. Taking the breath in and out of the mouth is an intense process and gets energy moving in the chest. It is more likely to activate birth and childhood memories and this needs one-to-one attention and love. Taking the breath in through the nose and out through the mouth is less intense and allows the energy to move into the brain rather than the chest, facilitating an expansion of consciousness. Together with the physical movement that is a part of my group work, this type of breathing gets energy moving throughout the body and so enables a letting go through body expression.

● ●

Try this.

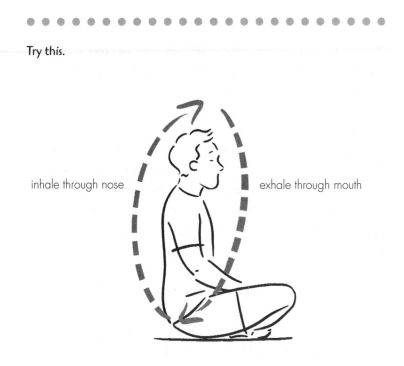

inhale through nose   exhale through mouth

CIRCLE OF BREATH

Sit upright, close your eyes and relax your body.

Take a deep breath in through your nose and then a deep breath out through your nose. Stay relaxed and keep the breath continuous so there is no pause between the in-breath and out-breath. Feel the breath filling your chest and your belly too; feel the whole body breathing. Continue for a minute or two until you are comfortable with this.

Now do the same but breathing in through the nose and out through the **mouth**. Keep the jaw relaxed. Let the whole body breathe and continue for a minute or two until you are comfortable with this.

Now imagine you are drawing a circle with your breath. As you inhale through your nose, draw the breath from the base of your spine up to the crown of your head. On the exhale, release the breath down the front of your body, closing the circle at the base of your spine again. Keep the breath relaxed, focusing on drawing the breath up intentionally and just letting the exhale go. Keep the breath continuous and smooth, like a circle.

Continue for as long as you feel comfortable.

You may start to feel a tingle in your body or become light-headed – this is just energy moving. Just be aware of these sensations and RELAX! Just breathe for as long as you feel comfortable and then stop and lie down for a few minutes until the energy dissipates.

● ●

● ●

This is a variation of the 'Circle of Breath'.

Cleansing Breath

Sit upright, eyes closed, body relaxed.

Create a circle of breath as before.

Now bring your awareness to any parts of the body that feel tense or tired. Direct your breath to these points and imagine this stuckness dissolving. On the exhale, imagine this negativity leaving your body with the breath. Keep doing this until your body feels clear.

Do the same with any uncomfortable emotions that you may become aware of.

Do the same with any heavy or negative thoughts that you may become aware of.

Continue until you feel light and clear.

● ●

Holy Communion

Breath is the key to wholeness. By bringing awareness to how we breathe, we become aware of where there is a separation in our natural state of wholeness. We are all both physical and spiritual beings and our quest is the journey back to this remembrance. But because we have fallen from this state of grace, we live mostly in a state of separation. It is the ego, bolstered by our history, our conditioning and our culture, that stands in the way. By bringing awareness to our breath, we start the process of moving beyond the ego. **Breath heals the separation**.

Just watching how we breathe is the start of the journey. Every in-breath we take tells the story of who we are. The in-breath shows us how we take in life, it is how we gather in the world around us, it is an act of intention, it is our will. To inhale is to take in energy and convert it to Matter, it is the action that initiates the process of converting *prana/chi* into the biological events that sustain life: it is an act of creation. The pattern created by our in-breath shows us the pattern of our desire for life.

An incomplete in-breath shows us where we contract away from life. If our in-breath is weak and shallow, then our will to truly live and experience life in all its manifestations is also weak: maybe life has hurt us and now we are afraid, maybe we feel we do not deserve to have what we want and now we live life on the surface, disinterested and devitalized. If our in-breath is urgent and we almost gasp for air, trying to take in as much as we can as fast as we can, then we want to live life fully, we are greedy for all it can give us. But because we have a basic mistrust, we are not sure that our needs will be satisfied and so we have an urge to impose our will as strongly as we can. In contrast, a balanced in-breath is one that is strong yet relaxed, one that activates the tender energy of the chest as well as the creative energy of the belly, one that inspires us to live life totally!

The out-breath shows us how we let go in life, how we go with the flow, how we surrender. To breathe out is to complete the act of creation by returning Matter to energy: in other words, what has been processed on the physical level can now be given up to the unseen world. A balanced exhale is one that is totally relaxed, without effort, it happens naturally. A balanced breath is also one that is complete, so that all the breath is returned until an inhale automatically follows. When there is an attempt to push the breath out in any way, this shows that we are trying to get rid of something, to push away our experience of the world: it is bad, it is dirty, it hurts, we don't want it. When the out-breath is only partial, then we are unable to let go, we feel the need to control life. The out-breath shows us where we hold on, where we are in fear. When the out-breath is incomplete, then so is the inhale and so we set up a struggle.

A healthy, balanced cycle of breath is one where our will and our ability to surrender are equal, where we can both receive and release, where we trust that life will take care of us because breath happens naturally. A full cycle of breath is one that reaches all parts of our being, where the whole body breathes, where feelings move through us freely and thoughts are like passing clouds. To breathe fully is to know that beneath all the turbulence is a stillness that is constant. Life is not 'this' or 'that': it simply 'is'!

Breathing is a communication with our deepest self. By bringing awareness to the breath, we get to know ourselves. By watching the inhale and the exhale, you see the ego's games: you don't need to understand, just watching is enough, just being aware. By watching, you are allowing yourself to move into the present moment. Eventually, with practice, you will have moved so much into the moment, that the ego, the thinking mind, will be transcended – have you ever tried focussing on your breath and thinking at the same time?! Here, in the Now, you communicate with your real self, not who you think you are. It is here in the Now that consciousness expands. It is here that you enter the gap between thoughts, it is here that you get in touch with that part of you that is Spirit.

● ●

Try this – you can do this anytime, anywhere.

Stop and Breathe!

Wherever you are right now just stop and become aware of all the thoughts that are running through your mind.

Now turn your attention to your breath, watching it enter your body through the nostrils, move into your chest, down into your belly and watch it move back out of your body through your nostrils and into the surrounding air.

Are you thinking or breathing?

● ●

To breathe is to inspire: the word 'inspire' comes from the Latin *inspiritus*, which means to be full of life, full of vigour, full of Spirit or soul. Similarly, in Greek the word for breath is *pneuma*, which means soul/Spirit. In the biblical story of Creation it is said that ' ... the Lord God formed man of the dust of the ground, and breathed into his nostrils the breath of life; and man became a living soul.' To be inspired is to be filled with Spirit, to be fully alive. To breathe is to communicate with your deepest being. Every time you breathe, you move between form and formless: in the gap between the two is your essence. Here, in this gap you can unlock the secrets of your soul. Here, in the silence of the Now you enter other worlds, unseen dimensions: breath is a communication between Matter and Spirit.

A complete balanced breath comes from the heart: it is here that Matter and Spirit unite. It is no accident that the chemical exchange of molecules occurs in the heart and lungs: it is here that energy is converted to Matter and vice versa. The heart is the place of wholeness, where giving and receiving are in an endless cycle of continuity. It is in the heart that we are most wounded, it is the heart that gets broken, and it is the heart that bursts open with joy and love: it is in the heart that we embrace the whole of Existence. When we breathe, we take in the same air that has been breathed in and out of every living creature that ever existed since the beginning of time. Through our breath we are One with all that exists. Breath connects us all. This is the most intimate act – no wonder the heart is the place of intimacy.

Breathing is an act of love, a Holy Communion with Existence, with God/Goddess, with All That Is.

● ●

Try this Tantric exercise. You can do it with a partner, someone you are close to (same or opposite sex, it doesn't matter!), someone you are comfortable with, someone you trust – or you can do it alone:

inhale

gaze into each
others eyes

inhale

MELT INTO ONE

Melt into One

Sit upright, either face to face with a partner or in front of a mirror. Keep your eyes open, relax your body and get in touch with your breath.

Do the Circle of Breath with the inhale through the nose and the exhale through the mouth. If you are doing this with a partner, make sure your breath is synchronized. Keep your eyes soft-focus and your face relaxed.

Watch the feelings and sensations that arise – you may become aware of layers of resistance – just keep breathing and watching.

Watch how boundaries melt and you become one.

● ●

Chapter 12

Awaken the Serpent

*The rainbow serpent, upon whose back I had ridden into
the very core of my being, was going to turn on itself now
and swallow its own tail.*

MERILYN TUNNESHENDE

Kundalini Power

Forget 'girl-power' – or 'boy-power' for that matter – Kundalini-power is
where it's at! Kundalini is your powerhouse, your creative life-force. We all
have it, for without it we could not function in the world. It is your 'oomph',
your driving force; it powers your whole being. Every action you take is an
act of creation and Kundalini-energy is the source of this creative process.
Kundalini is *prana/chi* in its densest form and it sits at the base of the spine,
in the seat of your pants so to speak. It is literally **the seat of your life-force**!

Every act of creation is sexual. From the merging of opposites, something
new is always born. When the polarities of male and female come together,
there is an explosion of energy, which has the power to move Heaven and
Earth. From making a cake to making a masterpiece to making a baby,
creating anything involves the activation of sexual energy. From the joining
of sperm and ovum at conception to the creation of the universe out of the
Void … it's all one Big Bang!

Kundalini is sexual energy, it has the power to create: here lie the seeds of male and female energies waiting to be activated. Kundalini is potential energy waiting to be released: here is the seed of awakening. When Kundalini is activated, it has the power to give birth to consciousness. This is not consciousness in its original form, or disembodied Spirit, but consciousness fully manifested in physical reality, that is, in the body, right here, right now. Of course, Kundalini is within each and every one of us. It is just a matter of how conscious we are. The more Kundalini is activated, the more conscious we are and the more creative energy we have at our disposal. The more creative energy, the more fuel we have to power us, and so the more alive we are, the more awake. When we are not conscious, we live non-creatively: in other words, we are like robots, asleep, just carrying out daily tasks. True creativity comes from being spontaneous, being able to respond rather than reacting blindly, being able to make conscious choices. True creativity means that life is fun, we can play the 'cosmic game' rather than getting caught up in deadly seriousness.

Kundalini is like a serpent, coiled up asleep at the base of the spine. Here, Kundalini is likened to Shakti, the female aspect of Existence, the Goddess, the life-giving force that animates everything: she is the force of manifestation. Here, Kundalini waits to be awakened and then she will spring up, releasing her power. Since female contains male within her – as Goddess contains God – this awakening activates a polarity of energies, female and male, which rise up the centre of the spine. This is the dance of Shakti and Shiva. Shiva is the male aspect of Existence, pure consciousness, the unmanifest, the Source. When Shakti reaches the crown of the head, she merges fully with Shiva to create a perfect balance of male and female energies. This is enlightenment. The journey from bottom to top is the journey

145

of life. The journey is the transformation of raw sexual energy to the light of awareness.

Kundalini is the Serpent-Goddess and the serpent is a symbol of duality: she is both female and male, both dark and light, both matter and consciousness. The journey we take starts at potentiality, moves through duality and finally merges with unity. The snake is also a symbol of fertility and transformation; hence the awakening of Kundalini initiates the journey from sex to super-consciousness. And just as a snake periodically sheds its skin so that it may grow, so does the path of awakening require us to let go of the old so that we may move forwards on our path in life. The snake is a powerful symbol of creative and healing power and the image of two snakes intertwined is an ancient one. This symbol of caduceus, with the two snakes indicating the male and female energies rising up the central energetic core of the body – also known as the *Sushumna* – was seen in ancient Egypt in association with Thoth the God of Divine Communication, in Greek mythology as the magic rod of Hermes the Messenger of the Gods, and in the Tantric texts of ancient India. Today, it has been adopted by the medical profession as a sign of health. The serpent symbolizes the regenerative powers of the self, the transcendence into immortality and the journey to our divinity.

The awakening of 'the sleeping serpent' activates the dance of polarities so that as Kundalini rises, the female and male energies move away from each other and move towards each other again. The points at which they meet are vital centres of consciousness. These are vortices of energy, which have the power to transform. Here, the male and female energies unite in an act of creation. These are the seven major **chakras** – there are a number of

KUNDALINI RISING

minor ones too – which form a map of our journey through life. Each chakra has a female and male counterpart. The female part receives energy, draws energy in to itself; the male part gives this energy out and circulates it around the chakra system. As female and male merge and blend, they spin a vortex of energy, hence chakras are frequently called 'wheels of energy'. When the female and male aspects are balanced, then that energy centre is also balanced and we remain healthy and whole. When it is out of balance, our health reflects this imbalance.

The chakras are where mind and body meet: they are entry-points into the quantum body and so they are keys to our well-being. On a purely physical level, the chakras correlate with nerve ganglia and with the endocrine system (the collection of glands which regulate important physiological processes by releasing hormones). On a physical level too, the *Sushumna* correlates with the spinal cord and the energy generated by the chakras radiates out through the body's energy channels, the meridians/*nadis*. In addition, the male and female polarities are thought to be related to the two brain hemispheres, so that the male correlates with the left hemisphere and the female correlates with the right. It is when these brain hemispheres are synchronized or balanced that transcendence is attained.

The chakra system is not something separate from us: it is who we are, the totality of our being. It is every single bit of us: it is the physical, emotional, mental and spiritual. Whether we are aware of it or not, it is there. Each of the seven chakras corresponds to a particular aspect of our physical nature, our emotionality, our thought processes and our spiritual understanding. Each chakra relates to a particular quality of life, a particular aspect of human experience. Chakras are not some esoteric invention, but a fact of life. If we take notice of them, they will help us to understand ourselves. Many diverse cultures across the ages have drawn on chakra wisdom, from the ancient Egyptians to the ancient Indians to the Native Americans. There is also a correlation between the chakra system and the seven Christian sacraments as well as the 'Tree of Life' of the Judaic Kabbalah. The rise of consciousness through the chakra system is also very like the development of an aware ego (discussed in Chapter 3). Whilst this knowledge has been lost for many years, today we see it being increasingly acknowledged by some parts of the medical profession.

We do not have to able to see chakras, but we can feel their effect on our well-being and so we bring awareness to our lives. When a chakra is blocked and energy becomes unbalanced, we exhibit the negative side of this quality. When energy flows freely, we exhibit the positive side.

● ●

Table of Chakras and Qualities

CHARKA • Location • Gland • Body parts	BALANCED	UNBALANCED
BASE • Base of spine/perineum • Adrenal glands • Feet/legs/rectum/spine/ bones/immune system	Good overall physical health Emotionally stable/grounded Practical/able to get things done Feeling 'at home' and safe in the world	Poor physical health Emotionally unstable/ ungrounded Out of touch with reality Feeling disconnected
SACRAL • Lower abdomen • Ovaries and testicles • Pelvis/sexual organs/ bladder/large intestine/ circulatory system	Healthy sexuality Sensual/pleasure in own body Creative Able to feel emotions Sense of peace and harmony	Sexual dysfunction Disgust/shame of body Creatively blocked Over-emotional/lacking in feeling Insecure/fear of aloneness
SOLAR PLEXUS • Middle abdomen • Adrenals and pancreas • Digestive system/liver/ gallbladder/spleen	Healthy digestion Trust in self Decisive/courageous Respectful Sense of personal power Joyful and abundant	Poor digestion Indecisive/fearful Lack of self-worth Selfish Out of control temper Depressed/lacking vitality

HEART

- Centre of chest
- Thymus gland
- Lungs and heart/chest/ arms and hands

Compassionate	Uncaring
Love of self and others	Lack of self-love
Able to feel pain and joy	Stuck in hurt
Balanced	Lack of direction
Faith in life	Confusion

THROAT

- Centre of throat
- Thyroid and parathyroid
- Neck/trachea/teeth/ mouth

Able to speak up for self	Lack of self-awareness
Clear communication	Sense of isolation
Sensitive to others	Insensitive
Sense of personal authority	Self-righteous

THIRD EYE

- Centre of forehead
- Pineal gland
- Eyes/ears/nose/nervous system

Expanded awareness	Mental confusion
Clarity of purpose	Limited view of life
Spiritual connection	Lack of purpose
Wisdom	Scepticism

CROWN

- Top of head
- Pituitary gland
- Cerebral cortex

Able to experience bliss-states	Alienation
Faith in the Divine	Lack of meaning in life
Cosmic connection	Unable to let go into 'being'

● ●

Chakra Journey

The journey through the chakra map starts at 'base camp', at the very root of the spine. Here, we develop our basic sense of self, our foundation. This is raw, undifferentiated creative sexual energy, it gives us our will to live, as well as our connection with our ancestors, family or tribe. At the second level, in the belly, this energy becomes differentiated into duality: who 'I am' and who 'you are'. Here, we learn how to relate to the world around us. We learn about rhythms, the constant flux of energy as we get close and move away from the outside world, the flow of inner feelings. As we move up to the third level, the solar plexus, we experience our authority according to what is right or wrong for us. At the fourth level, in the heart, we move beyond right and wrong to a place of unity, where joy and pain co-exist. Here, we learn about compassion, about opening our heart to the world. The fifth stage, the throat-centre, is where we learn to find our voice, to speak our truth. At the sixth level, the centre of the forehead or 'third eye', we develop inner vision, insight and clarity. Finally, at the seventh level, the crown of the head, we move beyond time and space to a place of limitlessness, stillness and absolute awareness. Here, we have transcended the 'I am' to become All That Is.

● ●

This is a simple exercise to bring awareness to your energy centres, to your chakras.

Kundalini Journey

Sit upright, close your eyes, relax your body and get in touch with your breath.

Bring your awareness down to the base of your spine, just where your body makes contact with the ground beneath you, and breathe into this space. Let your breath fill up the whole lower part of your body, from the base of the spine to your feet. Allow yourself to become aware of any sensations and feelings here. It may feel warm, cold, light, heavy, or you may see a colour, or whatever – just allow any impressions to come to your consciousness without censoring.

Do the same with the area between the base of the spine and your navel.

Do the same with the area between the navel and your diaphragm just beneath the ribs.

Draw the breath up to the chest and do the same here, receiving sensations and impressions from the heart, arms and hands too.

Draw the breath up to your throat and do the same here.

Now breathe up to the middle of your forehead and let your breath fill your whole head – be aware of the sensations and impressions.

Now draw the breath up to the crown of the head and do the same.

Now just let your awareness drop back down to the base of your spine, become aware of the weight of your body on the ground beneath you and slowly open your eyes.

● ●

The natural progression from level one to seven is a lifetime's journey, from birth to old age, from the first breath we take to claim our place in the world to the last breath we take where we merge back into Spirit. It is also the soul's journey over lifetimes of experience in its quest for enlightenment. On an everyday level, though, we do not always progress smoothly through the stages. We come into this life with certain predispositions, having learnt or not learnt the lessons of previous incarnations. Our task in this lifetime is to become aware of where we are blocked, to rebalance ourselves so that energy may flow freely. The lessons, obstacles and opportunities that our current life presents, are clues to where we need to redirect our energy.

Each chakra is intimately linked to all the others and a block in one will affect another. For example, if energy is blocked at the first level, we become too earthbound, overly concerned with the material aspect of life, accumulating possessions as if our very life depended on it. In this case, it may be difficult for us to get in touch with our higher self, the part that can see the wider picture, and so we lose our spontaneity and creativity. On the other hand, if the higher centres, such as the third eye and crown, are open but energy is getting stuck lower down, say, at the throat level, then we become too 'cosmic'. We are able to channel divine inspiration but unable to put ideas into action, and so we live with our 'head in the clouds'. Chakra imbalances are simply stuck energy. By bringing awareness here, energy will start to move. When Kundalini is awakened, like a serpent of fire, she burns away blocks and clears away toxicity. Kundalini is the great purifier, she is the awakener of consciousness and each chakra is like a rung on the ladder: I call this the **Seven Steps to Heaven**.

The activation of Kundalini is the beginning of spiritual emergence. Much has been said in traditional scriptures about the dangers of Kundalini. Whilst there is a truth here in that the awakening of such a powerful energy can create havoc in your life if you are unprepared, the scaremongering about Kundalini is just not relevant to today's fast-changing world. We are living in times of heightened evolution, times when for most of us change is a part of everyday existence. These days, it seems that Kundalini is being activated anyway, that we are being pushed by Existence to climb the ladder!

The growing number of people involved in self-development is an indication of this. More and more people are breathing, healing, meditating and dancing themselves to heaven! More and more people are becoming attuned to energy, whether it be through yoga, chi kung, reiki or Tantra. We are being given a huge wake-up call! Kundalini is a natural force that we need only become aware of. The danger lies in not being aware. Kundalini activation is great, but what we do with it, how we integrate it into our lives can be problematic. In particular, the large-scale unconscious use of recreational drugs can activate Kundalini and spark off a spiritual emergency: it is here that guidance and grounding are crucial. Unfortunately, this is precisely where it is missing!

Again, as when I work with the breath, I sometimes see a lot of resistance when I work with chakras. I am eyed with suspicion, as if I am talking about something mysterious and possibly dangerous. Just the mere mention of the word 'chakra' creates such a mistrust in some people, as if we are dabbling in the occult, as if the secrets of the soul are about to be revealed. At the other extreme, some people get off on the idea that we are playing with the esoteric, that it is something really spiritual and therefore special.

Working with chakras is simply working with energy – and energy is just a fact of life. Energy exists whether you believe in it or not; energy exists irrespective of what you call it. Every time you go walking or jogging in the nearest park, every time you squat down to reset the video because the remote isn't working ... every time you are opening the energy centre of the first chakra. Every time you want to rush out and fly the flag when England score a goal, every time you experience the euphoria of being one big family when you dance in a sea of sweaty bodies at a music festival, every time a rush of pride floods through you when your son/daughter/niece/nephew takes their first step/speaks their first word ... every time you are experiencing the energy of the first chakra.

Every time you wiggle your hips on the dance-floor, make thrusting motions in the throes of passionate lovemaking, or rub your lower belly because it feels good, you are in touch with the energy of the second chakra. When you feel irresistibly drawn to someone, when you feel abandoned by someone, when you are gutted because you lost all your savings on the stock-market, or when you have just made loads of money on a lucrative deal ... this is second-chakra energy.

Every time you run as fast as you can for the bus because you will get on come what may, every time you do those damned sit-ups in the gym, every time you chop wood (do you ever?) ... you are activating third-chakra energy. When you have the courage to take a risk even though it feels scary, when you put your creative projects into action and follow them through to the end, when you can laugh at yourself and the bitter-sweet lessons of life ... these are third-chakra energy.

Do you get the picture? Every aspect of life is related to the movement of energy. When I work with chakras – and increasingly I do not label them that – I simply describe the energy. As always, the first port of call is the physical body. Through movement and awareness, you get in touch with the movement of energy through the body. Since physical energy is the densest, it is the easiest to feel. For example, if you close your eyes and very slowly make circles with your hips, you will start to feel a warmth in your pelvic area. If this doesn't work, try closing your eyes and rubbing your lower belly for a while. As you get more sensitive to energy, as you start to fine-tune your awareness with practice, then you can feel this energy on an emotional level. For example, you may start to feel a range of emotions, from desire to disgust, from satisfaction to repulsion. At more and more subtle levels, you may experience inner visions, colours and sounds, and at even more subtle levels you may gain insights into certain aspects of your life.

Adding breath awareness to the equation increases the movement of energy. I use simple but specific breathing techniques to add power to the whole process. The breath activates the movement of energy and starts to move through blocks and resistances, clearing the path so to speak. If you then add a visualization, the process is even more powerful. A visualization is a technique for moving energy on the thought level – **energy always flows where attention goes**. So, if you imagine – and this simply means bringing your attention to something in a very specific way – drawing in, say, energy from the Earth and up your spine, then that's exactly how energy will move.

Movement, breath and visualization is a potent mix for initiating transformation, for activating Kundalini.

● ●

Here are some of my favourite recipes for 'awakening the serpent'.

SHAKE HER AWAKE!

This is a wonderful exercise. Do it as often as you like, for as long as you like. The longer you do it, the more sublime the experience! Put on some music – something with a fast rhythm, something that inspires you to shake:

Shake Her Awake!

Stand with your feet shoulder-width apart and planted firmly on the ground. Close your eyes and soften your knees, relax the anus and genitals, relax the shoulders, keep the arms loose, neck and face muscles relaxed too.

Start circular breathing, in through the nose and out through the mouth. If you like, you can add the visualization of drawing energy up from the Earth and in through the soles of your feet, up your legs and into the base of the spine. Imagine this breath is rousing the sleeping serpent here. Keep drawing the breath up the spine to the crown of the head. On the exhale, allow the breath to just wash down the front of your body, back down your legs and through your feet back into the Earth.

When you feel ready, start shaking. Start at the base of the spine, as if you are shaking the serpent to wake her up. Keep your knees soft like springs and your feet firm. Allow this shake to move up your spine and through your body. Stay loose, let the whole body shake, tremble like a leaf in the wind ... become the shaking ... keep breathing!

Continue for at least 10 minutes and up to 30 if you can. Enjoy!

Allow your breath to come to normal, your body to come to standstill and lie down for a few minutes.

You may feel as if your boundaries have melted, or you may feel surges of energy move through you, or you may even experience inner visions, or a blissful feeling. At the end, you may feel a timeless quality, a feeling of stillness and peace.

This is an adaptation of Osho's 'Kundalini Meditation'. It is also a variation of the 'spontaneous movement' exercise in chi kung.

● ●

● ●

This exercise may be a little more intense than the previous one – take it easy!

Seven Steps to Heaven
Stand as before, close your eyes and stay loose and relaxed.

Bring your awareness to the area around the base of your spine, anus and genitals. Breathe into this space in and out through the mouth ... keep the breath quite short and sharp letting any sounds to come out on the exhale. At the same time, let your pelvis rock backwards and forwards. Just stay aware of any feelings and sensations here. Do this for a couple of minutes.

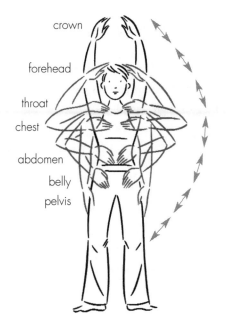

crown
forehead
throat
chest
abdomen
belly
pelvis

Now bring your breath into the navel area and allow your hips to swivel and rock in time with your breath.

Repeat this procedure for the following areas – abdomen between navel and diaphragm, chest, throat, centre of forehead, crown of head – each time keeping the breath short and letting out any sounds, spending a couple of minutes in each section. Throughout keep the whole body loose with special attention to the part you are breathing into and allow your arms to emphasize the movement. You may find that your arms naturally rise to the level of the chakra you are breathing into – this is good so allow it to happen! As you move up

161

through the chakras, allow any sounds to come out on the exhale –
you will find that the tone becomes higher as you move up.

When you reach the top, gently allow the breath to come back to
normal and the body to come to a standstill and bring your awareness
back to your feet – get grounded!

This is an adaptation of Osho's 'Chakra Breathing Meditation'.

● ●

In my workshops, I almost always include one of these exercises as a
warm-up. Activating the raw power of Kundalini energy provides the
groundwork of my 'Moving into Ecstasy' workshop. It is like turning on the
ignition in a car. When I first created 'Moving into Ecstasy' I knew nothing of
chakras. Yet on an intuitive level, I knew that energy moves upwards from
Earth/Goddess/Shakti to meet the downward-flowing energy of
Heaven/God/Shiva. I knew that as the two energies met in the body, they
created a dance, a dance of male and female, dark and light, passive and
active, push and pull. I knew this because I had experienced these energies
dancing in my body, weaving in and out of my life. When I danced, my
feet were rooted deep in the Earth, whilst my mind flew high above the
clouds. In between, my dance was a healing journey through all the aspects
of my Self.

This was the journey through my chakras; this was **Kundalini rising**. Now I
share this dancing journey with you.

3: The Journey

The journey of a thousand miles begins by finding your shoes.

OLD CHINESE PROVERB

Chapter 13

Dance Your Prayers

The more you dance, the more you sweat. The more you sweat, the more you pray. The more you pray, the closer you come to ecstasy.

GABRIELLE ROTH

The Ecstasy of Dance

To dance is to listen to the rhythm of your heartbeat and follow the pulse of life deep within your bones, to flow with the current of your feelings and let yourself be moved, to surrender to the passion of the moment and take flight into freedom. To dance is to resonate with the core of your being, vibrate with the hum of creation and express the uniqueness of your soul. To dance is to be fully alive, fully awake and filled with Spirit ... **to dance is to be ecstatic**!

People all over the world and throughout the ages have danced for healing, for wholeness, for holiness. Dance has been a part of the traditions of indigenous cultures for millennia. From the ghost dancers of the Sioux to the trance-dancers of Umbanda to the whirling dervishes of the Sufi, dance has been used as a way to move into an altered state of consciousness, a way to transcend mundane reality and connect with the Spirit world, a way to experience the magic of ecstasy. From the Dionysian rites of Minoa to the Fire Dance of the Navajo to the Love Dance of the Nubia, dance has been recognized as a powerful tool for healing and initiation through the creation of ritual and ceremony.

Dance is probably the oldest spiritual path to wholeness known to humankind: at the beginning of time, when all we had was the skin we live in, what else could we do but dance? Dance is the most natural activity in the world ... except for sex, and that too is a dance! Dance is an expression of the natural rhythm of the body, an outward extension of the inner dance of male and female energies. Dance connects us with the rhythm of life, the cyclical patterns of Nature, the heartbeat of Existence.

Many ancient mythologies speak of dance as the beginning of Creation. Perhaps the most widely known is that of Shiva Nataraja, 'Lord of the Dance', whose '... form is everywhere, all pervading ... Everywhere is Shiva's gracious dance made manifest ... He dances with Water, Fire, Wind and Ether. Thus our Lord dances ever in the court.' Shiva's dance creates the world and gives birth to the myriad forms of Existence; and Shiva's dance destroys all forms and returns them to the formless. This is the 'life/death/life' cycle that is the basic nature of the universe. Ancient humankind re-enacted this cycle by dancing, by imitating Nature. Through dance, the physical form is transcended, the self dies; and through dance, the spiritual being is created, we are reborn. By dancing, we move beyond fragmentation, beyond the many, and we experience unity, the One. The story of Creation is the dance of God.

In the pre-Christian Mystery rites, dance was an initiation to a higher level of being, a celebration of spiritual union after a long journey through darkness: this symbolized the psyche's development and the transition at various crucial life stages. This surrender to the divine by 'sacrificing' the body to the dance continued to be a feature right up until early Christianity, as seen in the 'Dance of Jesus'. Before the Mystery rites were banned as 'the work of the devil', the Disciples of Christ would re-enact the resurrection through ecstatic trance-dance. As Christ, the Son of God, Himself said: 'Whoever does not dance, does not know their immortality.'

To dance is to know the Beginning and the End. This is the great wheel of life, which, just like the serpent eating its own tail, the 'Ouroborus', symbolizes the union of male/yang/Shiva – the Serpent's tail – and female/yin/Shakti – the Serpent's mouth. To dance is to take part in the Great Mystery. The Christian mystic Gregory of Nanzianz said: 'Dance … for I believe that such a dance holds the mystery of walking in the sight of God.'

To dance is to know God, to enter the sacred circle of life and embark on the journey to the centre.

Journey to the Centre

The journey to wholeness is a dancing path, weaving in and out of light and dark, clarity and confusion, fear and love. Life is never static, nor does it follow a linear trajectory. In real life, there is no stable middle ground; there is no permanent security. Life cannot be controlled, mapped out, planned. To

167

believe so is one of the great illusions of the ego. To believe so is to set yourself up for a huge 'upset'. To hold onto this belief is to put a stranglehold on life, to choke all the mystery, depth and power out of Existence. It would be like holding your breath: you stop the flow of energy, numb your feelings and eventually die! As Joseph Campbell, the great mythologist, said: 'We must be willing to get rid of the life we planned, so as to have the life that is waiting for us.'

The only thing you can be sure of, is that life is impermanent – **everything changes**! Life is full of ups and downs, twists and turns, endings and beginnings: change is the nature of Existence. To be fully alive is to surrender to change, to allow each turn to take you to the next. Life is like a river, winding this way and that, changing direction and changing pace, but always flowing. The flow is sometimes slow, sometimes fast, often calm and occasionally turbulent, but always there is movement, always there is a pattern of change. We can resist this change, we can erect a safe barrier with our minds, but all we do is dam up the flow: we end up stagnating, restricting our life-force, becoming unconscious, asleep, stuck.

Only by allowing life to flow through us, do we surrender to the bigger picture of our soul's journey. Just as a drop of water from the sky returns to the ocean, so does the river of life return us to Source. To follow this flow with awareness is to take the journey back home to who we really are. When we become aware of the patterns we weave through life, we create our own unique dance. And this dance always takes us deeper into the centre of our being.

The pattern of my own life has taken me through endless cycles of changes. I have gone from the limelight of success to the darkest night of my soul, from the 'busy-ness' of running a business to the emptiness of being a 'nobody'. I have frantically climbed the career ladder, dwelled in the murky depths of depression, raced at top speed in marathons, and sat absolutely still for hours in deep meditation. Throughout, I have learnt that change is woven into the fabric of life – it is the way things are.

Each turn in the course of my life has led me to the next, somehow returning to the same place but from an expanded viewpoint, creating circles within circles – a spiral dance of self-discovery. Twelve years ago, when the call of awakening came amidst the darkest shadows of my despair, I walked away from the safe structures of the life I knew to embark on the uncertain search for my soul. As all the external trappings of my world fell away, an inner journey unfolded. I left behind all the material possessions I had accumulated: the nice minimalist flat, the fast posh car, the expensive designer clothes ... yes, it was the 1980s! I gave up the status I had so desperately strived for: the hard-earned qualifications, the burgeoning academic vocation, the successful teaching practice ... I thought I had it all! I walked out on the relationship I clung to so dearly: the romantic dream of perfect marriage and perfect kids ... who hasn't fallen for that, or some variation of it?!

With nothing to hold on to, I came face to face with who I am, not who I thought I was. When the wheel finally turned to transform a spiritual emergency into a spiritual emergence, another strand had been woven into the pattern of my life. Today, the wheel has turned again and I find myself teaching from a new perspective. And there are wheels within wheels, cycles within cycles. When, all those years ago, I dropped my obsession with bodily perfection to dedicate myself to matters of a more etheric nature, the wheel turned and I travelled out of my body and into the astral world of psychic phenomena. Today, I have come full circle back to my body, but from a higher perspective. Now, my body is the vehicle of my Spirit.

The turning point along this arduous road was when I discovered **the ecstasy of dance**. I have danced in sweaty clubs with thousands of people, alone in my tiny living room in London, in wide-open fields under the stars, on stages in front of thronging crowds, on deserted beaches watching the sunset on the other side of the world, precariously on the roof of my car, sublimely in a marble temple at the feet of a golden Buddha. I have danced in a psychedelic spacesuit, in full tribal costume and naked as a babe. I have danced my inner child, my power animal and my wild woman. Through dance I have broken the walls of my resistance, surrendered to both agony and ecstasy, and been bathed in the bliss of full body orgasm.

When I dance, I weave the pattern of my life, my unique story. When I dance, there is no right or wrong way … I simply allow the dance to happen. I simply follow the sensations, feelings and emotions as they arise in my body; I follow the urges, intuitions and inspirations as they arise in my soul. When I dance, my ego takes a back seat … there is no controller, no inner critic, no voice telling me what to do or not do. When I dance, I step into the unknown, I lose myself … I am just energy moving.

To me, dance is a path to self-awareness. When I dance, I get to know myself: I see where I am stuck and where I am in the flow, I see where I am asleep in my inertia and where I am awake in my ability to be fully present.

To me, dance is a path to higher consciousness. When I dance, I move out of my skin-encapsulated ego and extend myself to the whole of Existence. When I dance, every atom of my being vibrates with delight as my feet reach deep into the heart of the Earth and my head reaches up to touch the sky.

Dance is my teacher, my guru, my gift from the Gods.

Trance-end-dance

To dance is to get out of your head, into your body and on a moving journey to oneness. Amidst the movement, there is a point of stillness. At the centre of the cyclone is the eye of calm. To dance is to find the 'I' that is beyond the 'me'. To dance is to transcend the chatter of the mind, to find freedom from the limitations of the small self. To dance is to end the trance of the illusory world, to go beyond ego, to move into transcendence – or as I like to say 'trance-end-dance'. This is **trance-dance**.

To trance-dance is to dance yourself into an expanded state of consciousness. Here, you leave behind everyday thinking reality and enter the timeless world of Spirit. Gone are the petty thoughts, the restless round of worries, the judgements, the 'what ifs', 'buts' and 'maybes'. Gone is the neurotic obsession with the self you think you are, gone is the separation between 'me' and 'everything else', gone is the discomfort of self-consciousness. Now you are at one with yourself, at peace in the stillness of your being, complete in the ever-present Now. Here, you are connected to all that exists, all that has been and all that ever will be. Here, you see the greater reality, the truth of how things are.

In this place beyond time and space, you see with your inner eye, the 'I'. Here, you have expanded vision. In this place, you may see, hear, smell, taste and feel things that have been previously hidden to you. You may meet aspects of yourself that you had long forgotten. You may remember events in your personal history that have been deeply buried. For instance, an aspect we frequently shut away is the 'hurt child', the sensitive, vulnerable part of us that has been abandoned, abused, unloved. Another one is the 'magical child', that part of us that is playful, spontaneous, creative, wild and free-spirited.

When we deny these parts of ourselves by pushing them deep into our subconscious because the memory is too painful, we cut off from a part of our life-force: we become fragmented. By remembering, that is, bringing to consciousness, we re-member: we piece together, we make whole. Trance-dancing gives you the opportunity to re-member and in doing so you may have an emotional release – energy moves. This enables you to let go of the imprint of the trauma and so you reclaim a part of yourself. This is the same concept as 'soul retrieval' in Shamanic traditions, where aspects of the self or 'soul parts' are rescued or brought home from where they are stuck in non-ordinary realities.

Trance-dance is a safe way to experience powerful emotions because the physical movement keeps energy moving. To be able to contact primal feelings, which are otherwise locked away due to their pre-verbal nature, such as rage, aggression and desire, is deeply liberating. To be able to re-enact the 'life/death/life' struggle of birth is a powerfully creative process. Getting in touch with these feelings releases raw power and you may find yourself accessing dimensions that belong to the animal kingdom.

You may find yourself undulating hypnotically like a snake, prowling stealthily like a tiger, running with all the grace of an antelope, or flying with the serenity of an eagle. You may embody the spirit of this animal, feeling as if you have truly taken on its form, or you may meet this animal in some way and find it has some kind of wisdom to impart. In Shamanic cultures, these are known as 'power animals', guardian spirit-beings that protect and guide us. We can also see these as aspects of our own psyche, a part of our instinctual self that governs our survival instincts and our gut reactions: in other words, our 'animal nature'.

As you dance and sink deeper into your nature, you contact the primal force of Nature: sexual energy. Here you activate the driving force of creation. Here the awakening of passion may arouse the seducer/seductress within and the dance becomes an orgasmic experience. Such pleasure is unfortunately still a taboo in our culture: perhaps there is a fear of the intensity of power that is unleashed. Trance-dance provides a safe container or vehicle for the expression of such an intimate and beautiful experience. By bringing the focus inwards, you allow the male and female polarities to dance within you, you create a sacred space within your own body, just as the ancient matriarchal cultures honoured this alchemical union in sacred fertility rites.

And as you travel even deeper into the nature of your being, you may also get in touch with other beings: Nature spirits such as sylphs, elves and nymphs; higher beings such as cherubim, angels and archangels; and a whole pantheon of deities from the most blissful to the most wrathful. These are the transpersonal realms, the world of archetypes, mythology and the collective unconscious. Stan Grof, who is probably the world's foremost authority on consciousness research, calls them the 'holotropic realms': this is the place of quantum reality, which is beyond time and space.

Not everyone experiences such vivid visions when trance-dancing, and certainly not every single time. The images may not be clear; you may instead have fleeting sensations that contain the essence of these other realms, or you may simply be filled with coloured or white light. At times, you may experience waves of energy or find that it is as if your body has disappeared, that you are translucent. Or you may have a direct experience of Source, you may have arrived at the stillpoint where the emptiness of the moment is pregnant with potential: this is the Void, where absolute nothingness vibrates with the fullness of ecstasy.

You may not always be intellectually aware of what is really going on in the dance, but always there is a great healing that happens in trance-dance. It is not an analytical exercise but an experiential process. Trance-dance is a whole-brain activity: the shift is away from the rational time-encapsulated left brain hemisphere and towards the non-rational timeless right brain hemisphere. The visionary states of mystics, the religious revelations of prophets and the waking dream-states of Shamans are all signs of such a holistic brain-state.

Not only is there a shift from left to right, but there is also a shift from top to bottom. The emphasis on neocortical activity in the forebrain that is a sign of intellectual activity is reduced and both the limbic and visceral systems come into play. Located in the mid-brain and hind-brain, respectively, these deal with our emotions, our primal urges and our more primitive basic body functioning. The inner visions and experiences of trance-dancing make sense in the light of this change in neurophysiological functioning, if we accept the holographic nature of our universe. Since external manifest reality is a reflection of our inner unmanifest reality, then it makes sense that whole-brain activity and consciousness expansion and a sense of wholeness go hand-in-hand.

Trance-dance heals on all levels of our being. Trance-dance heals on the physical level because energy is moving, because both the physiological and the quantum mechanisms are accessed. The body is cleansed of toxins, tensions and traumas: it is re-energized, revitalized and ready to go! Trance-dance heals on the emotional level because there is a catharsis of stuck feelings, because the whole body-mind system is activated. Trapped hurts are remembered, forgotten feelings resurface and locked emotions are released. Trance-dance heals on the mental level because consciousness expands, because your receiver tunes in to a wider frequency. The mind drops its obsession with negative thoughts, suspends its habitual judgement, and is open to the greater cosmic flow. When all three levels of being are cleansed, then you are ready for healing on the spiritual level. **Trance-dance is an invitation to Spirit**, a surrender to the magic of transformation, a step on the path to wholeness.

The first move on the dancing path is always a step into the unknown. Dance is a surrender of the small self to the Greater Mystery. It is a statement of trust: trust that there is a universal power greater than you, trust that you will be carried to the place of wholeness. Dance is not a doing: it is an undoing, a letting go. The first step is to 'get out of your head' and come into the present moment ... and breath is the key that unlocks the power of Now.

In my teaching, I use a very simple repetitive breathing pattern called the **Breath of Fire**: this switches off the thinking mind and facilitates the transition to whole mind. There are a number of variations on this type of breathing, but I find the Breath of Fire the most effective and easiest to learn. Not only does this particular pattern increase oxygenation to the whole body, it also takes oxygen rapidly to the brain to facilitate an expansion of consciousness. It also acts like a mantra, a steady rhythm that synchronizes brain waves and enhances a holistic state of mind.

● ●

Try this for a few minutes. Make sure you are sitting or standing comfortably and close your eyes:

Breath of Fire

Take two short breaths in through the nose and then one longer breath out through the mouth. Keep the throat and shoulders relaxed, the rest of the body loose. The idea is that you take in as much oxygen as possible so you allow the breath to fill up your whole chest cavity. The exhale is a release and you can also make a sound if you wish.

You may start to feel a tingle or to feel a little dizzy – this is great! It shows that energy is moving. It may feel as if you are 'losing your mind' – great! Welcome the feeling – this is what you need to do!

● ●

I combine the rhythm of the breath with the rhythm of the drum. Music is an integral part of dancing, and the drum provides the most natural rhythm. All cultures use drums of one kind or another to communicate, celebrate and create ceremony. The first musical instrument is thought to have been a slit drum, basically a hollowed out piece of trunk split length-wise. Invented by the early matriarchal cultures, this was a symbol of the feminine, whilst the stick used to beat the drum was a symbol of the masculine. Together, these instruments represented the dance of polarities, the eternal rhythm of life. Even before this invention, we danced to the rhythm of our own bodies by stamping our feet, slapping our thighs and clapping our hands.

Different traditions that use dance as a spiritual practice employ a combination of breathing, drumming, chanting, repetitive movements and spinning: what they all have in common is a repetitive rhythm. The effect of a repetitive rhythm on the mind is to send it into trance: the rational mind switches off and consciousness is free to travel. Research has shown that the rhythm of the drum initiates 'theta' brain waves, the deepest trance-state, which enhances intuition, increases creativity, accelerates learning and also regenerates the brain through the release of certain chemicals. In my workshops, I use several drums to provide a steady beat, along with more chaotic beats. Together with several other instruments – such as guitar, didgeridoo, rattle, bells – a polyrhythmic landscape is created, within which the trance-dancer is safe to travel. Each instrument resonates with a different energy centre so that the whole spectrum is activated.

The Breath of Fire is a Kundalini-awakener. It will rev up your life-force, it will kick-start your consciousness, it will fire up your power. As the fire of transmutation moves through your body, it will activate your energy-centres, or chakras. This is a spiral dance, an unwinding of potential energy, an unfolding of latent power. This is a play of polarities, a meeting of male and female energies, a dance of the lovers within, a union of Spirit and Matter … **this is alchemy in action**!

Dance is a Tantric path, it is a big 'Yes', an invitation to life. Dance takes you to the threshold, it takes you to the darkness of despair, to the place of confusion and not knowing, and it takes you to the lightness of delight, to the place of freedom and absolute clarity. Dance takes you to the edge, to the place where you must either jump and trust that you will fly or fear that you will fall. If you dance with your whole being, if your surrender is total, then dance becomes a meditation. If you keep dancing, it takes you to the centre, the stillpoint … it is a direct route to Source! Dance is a moving meditation: 'You go on dancing and dancing and dancing and a moment comes of such ecstasy, of such extreme movement of energy, that in that movement the rock-like ego cannot exist. It becomes a whirlwind. The rock disappears and there is only dance. The movement is there but the mover is no more there … meditation has happened.' (Osho, *Sufis: The People of the Path*)

This is why I call my teaching method **Moving into Ecstasy**: through movement you come to a place where All Is One – and this experience of oneness is ecstasy! 'Moving into Ecstasy' is a method of ecstatic trance-dance that combines movement, breath and rhythm to take you into meditation – it is a fast-track to transcendence! Through the dance you lose yourself, you transcend your small self and you gain something infinitely more valuable: you become one with All That Is. I love this description by one of my class participants: 'The thing is to keep dancing and keep going and keep flowing and let the energy just keep coming and let the dance just keep coming … until the dance is dancing you.'

Trance-dance is not always blissful or ecstatic. Rather it is a process, and so you will step in and out of it. It is a practice, just like meditation: you simply watch what is happening rather than trying to make it happen. It is a path, and so trust is required: Spirit will do its work in its own time. All you need to do is to prepare the way and wait for God – it is a gift! All you need to do is empty yourself – and when you are empty, you will be filled with the divine. When you are at one with Existence, then all you can do is dance, because the divine is beyond words.

Dance is a path to healing because it awakens your life-force, your Kundalini power. Dance is a path to wholeness because it embraces all the parts of the self and takes you to the centre. Dance is a path to holiness because it is your communion with Source/the Divine/God/Goddess. 'Moving into Ecstasy' is my path to healing, wholeness, holiness … **it is my dancing prayer**!

Through trance-dance you are transformed. It is a path to transformation, or as I like to say – **trance-formation**!

● ●

Here is a 'how-to' of trance-dance. Make sure you have some room to move and nothing to bump into and that you will not be disturbed for, say, 20–30 minutes. Put on some music, preferably something with a tribal feel, but anything with a good repetitive rhythm will do.

Trance-end-dance

Stand with feet firm and rest of body loose and relaxed, close your eyes. Do the Breath of Fire for a couple of minutes or so.

As energy starts to move within you, as your rational mind starts to switch off, and as the music takes off, you will find that you will want to move. Just allow the movement to happen without controlling it; allow the body to express itself in any way it desires.

Keep doing the Breath of Fire whenever you remember to – you do not have to keep it up all the way through, just now and then. In particular, when you feel your rational mind coming in again to judge, analyse or criticize, then do the Breath of Fire; otherwise just keep breathing normally. As you get more used to trance-dancing, you can keep the Breath of Fire going for longer.

As the energy builds up, let yourself go ... dance as if you are drunk! Keep your feet firm so you do not topple over but let the rest of the body be as loose as possible, including the neck and head. Dance as if you are an empty vessel, just keep letting go. Go deep into your journey and enjoy!

At some point you may find that you have reached a peak or a place of stillness. You may feel like lying down now – just stop and drop to the ground in silence. This is an important part in order to ground yourself and bring you back gently into 'ordinary' reality.

Afterwards it is good to eat some warm food, have a hot bath or do something to pamper yourself and bring you back to Earth.

Note: if you suffer from epilepsy, a heart disorder, or if you are pregnant or menstruating, it is best not to do trance-dance as you may get overly dizzy. Personally, I have never met anyone who has had any adverse effects, but it's best to take care!

● ●

● ●

Here is what some of my class participants have to say about their trance-dancing experiences ...

> '*I am standing, waiting for the music to begin, my eyes closed. I am filled with anticipation, not knowing what to expect ... this is my first time. Then I hear the music ... a soft, haunting melody and then the slow but steady rhythm of a drum. I start the Breath of Fire, two breaths in and one breath out, my body is swaying gently side to side, the music builds up, my arms are creating patterns in the air, my head is rolling ... music, breath and movement have all melted into one. I am flowing, spinning, beyond time and space ... I do not know who or where I am. I am lost in a kaleidoscope of shapes, colours and sounds ... it is beautiful and oh so profound! Suddenly, bang! A rush of energy like electricity shoots up my spine and right into my brain, my head explodes into white light and I am showered in sparks coming*

out of the top of my head. I stand transfixed, rooted to the spot, my head tilted back, my whole body trembling with ecstasy. I am bathed in love and light, the most sublime orgasm I have ever had!'
MARY, TEACHER

'Beating drums and beating heart … I descend into darkness … I am in a cave and I am wild, ancient and free. I am a bear searching in the dark, sniffing and sensing so many things … what is it I am looking for? Something deep within me stirs and now I am a lion roaring loudly … out of my mouth comes a huge scream of pain, yearning, desire … I am stamping my feet to the rhythm of the Earth … now I am a barbarian slave dancing naked for the Tribal Chief, a dance of possession, seduction, fear and exhilaration. I fade into nothingness, engulfed by pure blackness and then blinding light … now I am a huge bird soaring over mountains and forests … I see so far, so clearly. I can hear the drums in the distance, they are getting closer now … I am back in my body as I know it, back in this large hall filled with so many people. I open my eyes and look around … everyone is still here yet somehow something has changed … bodies are glistening, faces are serene … a tremendous peace fills me.'
SALLY, AROMATHERAPIST

'Every time I do the trance-dance it is different but I always get a lot from it. I find it brings up a lot of "stuff" for me, issues rooted in my childhood that have caused me emotional problems. The dance helps me feel my emotions whilst putting them in

perspective. Somehow I can integrate my experiences without it being heavy "therapy". The main thing for me is to get over the "anxiety barrier" at the beginning where my mind is constantly judging and making excuses. Once I recognise this then I can let go and relax and this is when the dance becomes healing, as well as fun and good exercise! I always leave feeling lighter, clearer, refreshed and with a useful insight into my life.'
MARCUS, COMPUTER ANALYST

● ●

Tribal Revival

The body is an instrument of the divine. It is a holy vessel, for this is where wholeness is created. It is in the body that Spirit and Matter unite – this is the holy reunion of Heaven and Earth.

As the cosmic pendulum swings back towards the feminine perspective after an age of patriarchal rule, we see a rebalancing of male and female energies and a return to body honouring. After years of neglect and abuse, there is now a growing awareness of the benefits of looking after your body. As the demands of an urban lifestyle continue to escalate, the toll of stress is beginning to show. Consequently, there has been an upsurge of interest in holistic health matters over the past two decades. The importance of exercise, nutrition and relaxation is now widely espoused in glossy women's – and men's – magazines, in national newspapers and in a plethora of 'improve your life' books. Whereas 'alternative' used to be 'weird', today yoga, organic wholefood and healing massage are all filtering into the mainstream. Once seen as self-indulgent, today body pampering is recognized as being good for the soul. Health spas are now big business, holistic holidays are the in thing and luxurious feel-good health and beauty products line our shelves. In addition, there is an increasing acceptance of body-mind healing, from acupuncture to Ayurveda, as well as a more body-centred approach to many psychotherapies, such as Gestalt, Psychodrama and Bioenergetics. All this is an indication that we are getting back into our bodies.

And thank God/Goddess for that! For where would we be if we continued to remain stuck in our heads? A return to the feminine principle is timely in view of the growing global concern for the welfare of our planetary body, the Earth. The increasing tide of green awareness throughout the private and public sectors of society over the past two decades is indeed a healthy sign of rebalancing. Although we still have a way to go, 'organic', 'recycling', 'GM-free' and 'eco-friendly' are all terms that have infiltrated mass consciousness. In other circles too, the move towards an Earth-centred spirituality is picking up pace. The acceptance of James Lovelock's 'Gaia hypothesis' – the idea that the Earth is one huge living breathing organism – into some sections of orthodox science, the attempt to reinstate 'creation spirituality' by ex-Catholic priest Matthew Fox, and the spread of Pagan practices in the back gardens of suburban witches ... all these are indicative of a return to the Goddess.

Slowly but surely, we are making steps towards the resacralization of Nature, we are making a return to the sacred, to the sacredness of our nature. And there is nothing more natural than our own bodies. It is in our bodies that the natural rhythm of life is played out; it is in our bodies that the eternal dance of Shakti and Shiva is replayed over and over again. From time immemorial, we have danced to celebrate the sacred forces of Nature and now we return to this archaic path. Since Gabrielle Roth outlined her 'maps to ecstasy' in the late 1970s, the urban dancing tribe has steadily grown from city to city. Throughout modern culture we are witnessing a return to dance as a path to wholeness. From Biodanza to Barefoot Boogie, from Frank Natale's Dance of Life to Leo Rutherford's Shamanic Dance to Osho's dancing meditation Nataraj, more and more people are getting onto their feet and moving to the beat! More and more people, disenchanted with the stress of modern life, are turning to dance as a release from everyday pressures, as an outlet for pent-up emotions, as a form of therapy, as a path to healing. And as more and more people join the tribe, a sense of community grows too: here we can be totally ourselves and yet also join with others in a shared experience. The bottom line is that we all have rhythm in our souls!

It is no coincidence that dance exploded into the counter-culture scene of the mid-to-late 1980s. Here, amidst the conservatism of Thatcherite Britain (and later spreading across to the other side of the Atlantic) was a minor revolution in the making. Almost overnight, bankers and barrow boys, students and stockbrokers were dropping their identities together with their aspirations and getting back to their roots. Never before had so many people stomped in unison to a common beat.

I believe that rave culture erupted as an unconscious cry for freedom from the repressed youth of a patriarchal society. Here was an expression of the feminine principle in its raw form. Here, otherwise-estranged youngsters (and not so young ones!) found a commonality in their shared experience on the dance-floor. Here was a tribal situation, with the DJ as 'urban Shaman', the 'rhythm doctor' who transported them to other dimensions with trance-inducing beats. Here was an opportunity to let go and get out of their heads. This was a place where the joy of the moment could be celebrated. This was 'meditation for the masses', an experience of beingness for those who would otherwise not have known about such a reality. Here was a 'new religion' and as Matthew Fox says: 'These kids are showing us how to pray in a new way, which is also an ancient way – with fewer books and more dancing.'

Over the past decade, rave culture has become dance culture and has spread across cultures and generations, has gone from underground to mainstream, and has diversified and been commercialized. Whilst the scene has lost the purity of its original Earth-centred ethics, there is enough evidence to show that many of the original ravers have been turned onto the spiritual path. Personally, I have been sent many letters by people who have gone on to explore meditation, Shamanism, Goddess-worship and other disciplines as a direct result of their rave experience. I also have met many people over the years who now follow the 'healing dance' path. So many have been moved by the original rave rhythm and are still dancing to it in some form or another. Whilst today's mainstream dance scene bears little resemblance to its original form, nevertheless the beat goes on! Dance culture is now everywhere and certainly the current generation has been born into it!

For those like myself, brought up in pre-dance-culture days, the new trance-beat was a revelation! For me, it was on the dance-floor in the early days of the rave scene that music, movement and meditation first came together. It was here that I first became aware of the power of Spirit moving through my body. It was only several years later that I discovered Osho's 'active meditations': it was here, amongst hundreds of other 'dancing meditators' that I re-experienced the ecstasy of dance. Stomping my feet, waving my hands in the air, a big grin on my face, sweaty bodies gyrating and whirling around me … I could have sworn that Osho had invented the rave!

I remember a story someone once told me … I'm not sure of its accuracy nor of where I heard this, but it certainly grabbed my attention! It is a re-telling of the true story of the battle at Wounded Knee at the end of the nineteenth century when the Sioux of the North American prairies were massacred by the US Cavalry. It goes something like this … after the invasion of their homeland by the white man, the Sioux embarked on a mammoth 'Ghost Dance' ritual as a way of restoring harmony. It was prophesied by a Shaman that 'the dance of the ancestors would continue in white bodies' and so the tribespeople believed that the dance would provide protection. Could this mean that the 'white bodies' were the Ghost Dancers themselves or could this mean that their knowledge would somehow be passed on to their white brothers? Either way, it should have been a positive outcome. And so the dancers danced for days … and one by one they were all shot, one by one their bodies returned to Mother Earth whilst their souls awaited rebirth. Could this mean that the spirit of these Ghost Dancers has returned in the form of the dance scene that has swept across the Western world? I like this interpretation – it makes sense when you consider the growing awareness of the healing power of dance in urban society.

As more and more people get up and dance, so we see a reconnection with our archaic roots. As the pendulum swings back towards the feminine principle, so we see another cycle of change in the story of humankind. As each revolution of our planet takes us forward through time, so we move forwards on the path of evolution. As the pace of life speeds up and evolution accelerates, we fast-forward into the future.

As we turn the spiral of time to return to the long-ago past, we go 'back to the future' to re-create the present.

Chapter 14

Step Into the Circle

Hold to this timeless pattern
Throughout the time of your life,
Aware of the eternal cycles,
The essence of Tao.

ADAPTED FROM THE *Tao Te Ching*

Life Is a Circle

The nature of life is cyclical. Everything is always in motion, always changing, moving from one state of being to the next and then returning to complete a cycle. These cycles of change are the way of Nature, the rhythm of life. We can see this in the changing seasons, the waxing and waning of the Moon, the rising and setting of the Sun, the ebb and flow of the tide. We can also see this in the female menstrual cycle, the pulsing of our hearts and the fluctuations of our moods. Wherever life is natural, so is the rhythm cyclical.

These cycles of change are cycles of continuity: nothing ever stops, it just changes form. This is the 'life/death/life' cycle built into everything that exists. Just as a flower blooms, so it withers and becomes the compost for the next flower to bloom. Just as the rain falls and is soaked up by the soil, so moisture evaporates and condenses into clouds ready for the next rainfall. This cycle of change or continuity is actually a spiral: as each cycle is successfully completed, it is repeated at a higher level so that there is growth. This is the natural path of each human life and also of the development of the soul. As we achieve maturity and harmony at each stage of life, we can then move on to the next stage. When the life cycle is honoured, enlightenment comes as a natural and inevitable part of growing old and death is just an initiation into the next stage. The soul can then return to Earth to repeat the whole cycle, but from a slightly higher perspective, thus moving forwards on a spiral journey through time.

This is the natural way. Unfortunately, our modern world, with its emphasis on getting to the top of the ladder and achieving the highest goal, does not appreciate this spiral path of change. Frequently we remain stuck at a certain life stage, just because we have not honoured the need to move on. Many of us are stuck, for instance, as children in adult bodies, simply because we have not integrated and released childish emotional patterns. Our Western culture tends to be an adolescent one, with its emphasis on sexual experimentation, romantic love, pop-star idolization and baby-face beauty ideals … everyone seems to want to look and act like a teenager!

And many people are still clinging to the virility and stability of early adulthood even when we should be gracefully slowing down with old age. Unfortunately, our fast-paced culture has no place for the 'wisdom of the elders' – is it any wonder some old people retreat into senility. Senility is a perversion of an otherwise natural process. As in all cycles of continuity, as we approach death the psyche returns to the boundless state of infancy. But this time it is not the unconscious egolessness of early life, but rather the dissolution of boundaries that comes with transcendence of the ego through awareness.

Unfortunately, because the natural way is perverted in our modern culture, the end result is frequently the confusion, memory loss and childishness of senility. When we do not honour the changing life stages, we get stuck. When the psyche's development is not allowed to flow naturally, we return right back to where we started but with no forward motion: in other words, the spiral does not progress.

Nature clearly shows us the cyclical nature of life by exhibiting spirals visually. Wherever we look there are leaves curling, trees swaying and flowers unfurling. Birds swoop in beautiful sweeping arcs, butterflies flutter in complex circular patterns and fish swim in undulating wave-motion. This is in direct contrast to the linearity we see in the urban world. In the city we see straight lines, sharp edges and angular corners: tarmacked roads, grid-patterned streets, brick buildings, skyscrapers, tower blocks, square rooms, rectangular tables, and so on. The effect of all this linearity is to restrict our perception: the retina of the eye actually responds by narrowing its visual focus. In addition, the emphasis in Western culture on reading, writing, the performance of technical skills and ordered sequential thought, further limits our perception to left-brain analysis. In the West, we are conditioned to look, but we do not see. In Nature, the gentle curves and spiral structures actually relax the eyes: the retina widens and our vision softens. This soft-focus allows more light in to the eye and so the right side of the brain is also stimulated, giving us a more holistic view of the world. More light means an enlightened state of mind: when consciousness expands, we stand in our centre and see all the way around. This is the circle of life, within which the whole of Nature is encompassed, within which we acknowledge the all-embracing nature of wholeness.

The circle represents the eternal 'life/death/life' cycle; it is without beginning and without end – as is all that exists. The circle is a symbol of unity, of immortality, of holistic consciousness. The circle is a universal sacred symbol, an emblem of the Great Mystery. In Taoist philosophy, we see the Wheel of Existence represented by the well-known yin-yang symbol, in Tibetan Buddhism we see intricate *mandalas* depicting the different 'Bardo' stages or states of Heaven and Hell, and in the Pagan tradition we see the five-pointed pentagram, which creates a 'magic circle'. We also see circles of celestial beings painted on the ceilings of Christian churches, ancient monolithic sites of stone circles aligned to the motion of planetary bodies, and labyrinths mapping out the spiral path we must choose to walk both in life and death.

YIN-YANG

From the round dances of the ancient Greeks to the spiral dances of Pagans, and from the sun dance of the Native Americans to the whirling dance of Islamic mystics, the circle is the central theme. As a child I remember holding hands in a circle and dancing 'a ring, a ring of roses' … and I probably have – at least once – danced around my handbag!

The power inherent in the circle is demonstrated, as always, in Nature. Imagine the powerful forces within a whirlpool as it sucks you down to cold watery depths. This has been harnessed as 'vortex energy' by scientists looking for alternative sources of power. And how about the almost supernatural strength of wind when it is whipped up into a frenzy? We've all heard tales of destruction, devastation and destitution in the aftermath of a hurricane or tornado. The **Circle of Power** symbolizes the balance of natural forces, both externally in Nature and internally as in our inner nature. A particularly potent representation of this Circle of Power is the swastika, which is actually a cross within a broken circle. In the Shamanic traditions it is a symbol of self-empowerment, a sign of someone who has turned the wheel: in other words, someone who has become a 'master' of his own life, someone who has developed a high degree of awareness. In both the Chinese and Indian traditions it is a sign of good fortune, prosperity and long life.

It can also be seen in ancient Greece as a sun-wheel, in the Indo-Aryan tribes of Germany as the Cross of Thor and in early Christianity as a symbol of wholeness and power. It was later adopted by the Nazis … and look at the power unleashed there! Today, we see the circle used as a logo in the five circles of the Olympic flag uniting the five continents of the Earth, in worldwide campaigns such as the 'Breast Cancer Target Campaign' and in successful corporations such as the Orange telecommunications network.

CIRCLE OF POWER

We empower ourselves by stepping into the circle. The circle is a place of knowledge, a place of understanding: it is a map of consciousness. When we stand outside the circle, we are unaware, we do not yet know or understand ourselves. Here, we are victims of life, without conscious direction, still ruled by our conditioning, our habits, our negative programming. When we step into the circle, we start the journey of self-discovery, we get to know ourselves, we become conscious and to awaken to who we really are.

The circle has four cardinal points, just as there are four directions on Earth (north, south, east, west), four seasons in the year (spring, summer, autumn, winter), four pivotal positions of the Sun (dawn, noon, dusk, midnight), and four stages of life (infancy, childhood, adulthood, old age). All these divisions are based on the four elements in Nature: Earth, Water, Fire and Air. These are the four basic building blocks of life, the four basic aspects of the self, the four ways of being. Various traditions from around the world have developed maps of consciousness based on this division of four. In astrology, the zodiacal wheel has four fundamental divisions based on the four elements and related to personality characteristics. The earthy type is typically concerned with the material and practical aspects of life, the watery type is an emotional creature, the fiery type has a flair for creativity and drama, and the airy type lives in the world of ideas and ideals. In the psychoanalytic model developed by Carl Jung, the psyche too has been divided into four: sensation, feeling, intuition and intellect. Jung found that there are four psychological types, which favour one of these modes over the others.

In the Shamanic traditions, in particular the Native American way, the four elements are mapped out on the **Medicine Wheel**. This map is multi-layered, with the elements corresponding not only to topographical directions, seasons, Sun positions and life-forms (human, animal, plant, mineral), but also to levels of being (physical, emotional, mental, spiritual), life stages, personality characteristics, social structures and cosmic matters. In fact, you can overlay any facet of life on this map and it will give you the medicine you need; it will give you knowledge and understanding.

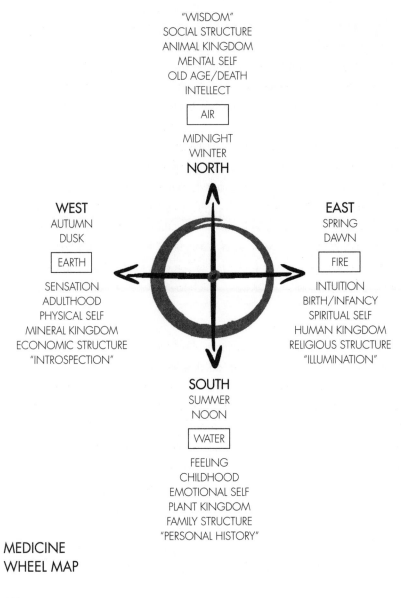

"WISDOM"
SOCIAL STRUCTURE
ANIMAL KINGDOM
MENTAL SELF
OLD AGE/DEATH
INTELLECT

AIR

MIDNIGHT
WINTER
NORTH

WEST
AUTUMN
DUSK

EARTH

SENSATION
ADULTHOOD
PHYSICAL SELF
MINERAL KINGDOM
ECONOMIC STRUCTURE
"INTROSPECTION"

EAST
SPRING
DAWN

FIRE

INTUITION
BIRTH/INFANCY
SPIRITUAL SELF
HUMAN KINGDOM
RELIGIOUS STRUCTURE
"ILLUMINATION"

SOUTH
SUMMER
NOON

WATER

FEELING
CHILDHOOD
EMOTIONAL SELF
PLANT KINGDOM
FAMILY STRUCTURE
"PERSONAL HISTORY"

**MEDICINE
WHEEL MAP**

It is important, as always, to remember not to confuse the map with the territory itself, not to confuse the tools with the journey. There are a number of variations of the wheel of life, depending on which tradition you look at. What is important is not so much the detail but rather the acknowledgement or the honouring of the circle, whatever tool you use, whichever map you read. What they all have in common is the division of four, the transition from one element to the next. What is important is the honouring of these transitions: these are the initiatory stages of life stages. In ancient cultures, ritual and ceremony were an important way of honouring these stages; this helps the psyche to move on and so we journey around the circle.

When we step into the circle of life, we start the journey of self-discovery. When we explore the four directions or four elements of the wheel, we start to understand what has shaped us, what makes us tick, what patterns we play out, what story we tell. By consciously undertaking this journey we release old patterns that hold us back, we discover who we are and we take a step into our power.

When we journey around the circle of life, we start at the place of personal history, which corresponds to the element of Water: this is the place of our inherited conditioning, our emotional wounds, our childish patterns. We then move on to the place of introspection, which corresponds to the element of Earth: this is the place where we find out who we really are, where we develop maturity. The transition involves a 'death' of some kind, a death of who we think we are, a leaving behind of the factors that shaped us and the limitations of our environment. If we hold on here, if we resist the change, then we remain stuck, we remain childish, immature. But if we have the courage to step forwards, we continue around the circle to the place of wisdom corresponding to the element of Air. Here we can step out into the world as true adults, able to share our knowledge and our clarity of being. Finally we can move on the place of illumination – the element of Fire – the place where we are aligned to our higher purpose and our greater vision. When we complete the journey we can stand in our centre. Here we are aligned to divine will. This is Spirit, the Source … the fifth element.

When we step into the circle of life, we are dancing our unique story, weaving the patterns that make us who we are. In the circle of life, we dance all our selves until we find our centre. This is our sacred circle, a place where we can die and be reborn, where we can be baptized anew. This is the place of ritual, a rite of passage that initiates us to higher levels of being. Ritual provides a structure for the playing out of unseen forces: it is like a crucible, a container for Spirit to enter our lives – a surrender to the power of Existence.

A Ritual for Our Times

A ritual is a rite of passage. It is a conscious decision for change, an intention for transformation, an invitation to Spirit. A ritual usually follows a set structure, a form, but within that structure there is room for Spirit to move: it is both a doing and an undoing. A ritual stands at the edge of form and formless, it is an entry-point into quantum reality, hence its power for change. A ritual is an affirmation of the mystery of life, a place of magic.

The first step in a ritual is our intention, a statement of our willingness to take part in this transformation: you could call this **a prayer for healing**. Once we have made this small step, we have opened our sacred circle, we have stepped into magical space. The second step is the **preparation**: here we get ourselves out of the way, we do whatever we have to in order to step outside of our ego-self, to let go of our many voices. Next is the **raising of energy**: without activating the primal force of creation, without harnessing the power of Existence, change cannot happen. So we need to access the flow of energy that is normally hidden from us, we need to move beyond the small self and step into the greater reality: this is the expansion into ecstasy. Now we can move into **surrender**: this is the third stage. Here, there is nothing to do: we have prepared the way and now we wait for the grace of God/Goddess. Now we are empty and wait to be filled by Spirit. The final stage is **grounding**: here we allow the energy to settle as we make the transition back to everyday reality. Now we can give thanks for this gift of healing and close the circle.

When I first conceived of 'Moving into Ecstasy', it was as a ritual, a sacred space for transformation. At the time I knew nothing of the power of rituals nor of the Shamanic maps of consciousness. And yet I had tapped into a universal knowledge with roots that went far back through my ancestry. As I stood on a hilltop overlooking the plains of Wiltshire, I felt the heartbeat of the Earth resonating beneath my feet. As I listened to the chaos of twenty or so drums all banging out their own tune, I heard the sweet voice of the Earth Goddess and I danced to her rhythm. I danced the mountains and the trees, I danced the rivers and the seas, I danced the Sun and the fire at the centre of the drumming circle, I danced the wind and the very air that I breathed. These were the four elements and I was creating my own sacred circle – this was my dancing prayer to the Goddess. I had tapped into something as ancient as time and I was guided to bring it bang up to date in my urban world … this was a **techno-Shamanic ritual**, the marriage of Shamanism and technological culture, a modern interpretation of an archaic and natural way.

Over time, I developed 'Moving into Ecstasy' into a healing journey, a ritual of **trance-formation**. The intention is for change, for healing and wholeness. In the preparation stage, you use the tools for catharsis, the techniques for clearing the way on physical, emotional and mental levels. To raise energy you activate the forces of Kundalini. And then you surrender into the trance-dance, you journey deep into your centre. Finally, you ground yourself and close the circle.

In 'Moving into Ecstasy', you dance the four elements, you move around the circle of life. Through movement, breath and awareness, stuck energy shifts and a healing happens. When you dance the four elements, you are working with the energy of the first four chakras: the base chakra relating to Earth, the sacral chakra relating to Water, the solar plexus chakra relating to Fire, and the heart chakra relating to Air. Here you explore the aspects of the self, this is your relationship with everyday reality, ordinary consciousness: this is basically the energy of Earth/Matter/Shakti. Once you have reached the heart centre, you move into the higher chakras. In my workshops, I do not specifically focus on the chakras at this point: it is here that the preparation has done the work, now it is time to surrender and allow a greater force to take over. If you have prepared totally, then the dance takes over. In the trance-dance, the higher energy centres are naturally activated and you journey through an inner landscape to the place of stillness. This is the place of transcendence, 'no-self', the Centre. This is the energy of Heaven/Spirit/Shiva. The sacred marriage is consummated in the heart: **this is the gateway to ecstasy**.

Dancing **the sacred circle of life** is not something just for those with an interest in ancient traditions: it is something for everyone! The dance of life does not stop just because we live in a modern world, the four elements are not just some Shamanic or Pagan construct: they are real forces that run through our lives, whether we know it or not. But we might as well get conscious about it; that's what we're here for on this lovely planet, to get conscious, to wake up!

Over the next few chapters I will show you how the four elements relate to your life and I will give you some tools that I use in my workshops to guide you on the map to higher consciousness, the path of trance-formation. As always, the four elements are felt in the body, so my focus is to get you 'out of your head and into your body' so you can get in touch with the sacred circle of life.

To make something sacred is to make it conscious, to awaken a deeper sense of reality, to come into the eternal present where magic happens. Non-sacredness is unconsciousness, it is robot-like actions, just mechanically doing things without really understanding why, without seeing the deeper reality, without touching the essence. Actually, **anything can be made sacred**, from sex to psychedelics to rock'n'roll to food to anything you can imagine … **all you need is a large dose of awareness!**

Chapter 15

Get Down to Earth!

> *Oh, for goodness sake get down off that crucifix, someone needs the wood.*

FROM THE MOVIE *'Adventures of Priscilla, Queen of the Desert'*

The Story of Earth

Earth is our Mother. We have sprung from the fertile womb of her creativity and are nurtured in the embrace of her physical body. Earth is our shelter, our home, our safe base amidst the vastness of the Universe. Earth is the ground that we walk on, the mountains that we climb, the bones that support us, the food that nourishes us. Through the fecundity of Nature, Earth expresses her unconditional love as she pours out her fertile riches in the myriad life forms that inhabit the planet. Through the complexities of Matter, she shapes our environment to inspire beauty and awaken in us a sense of wonder and awe.

Earth is the holder of an ancient wisdom: if we watch and listen carefully she will be our teacher in the ways of life. The cycles of Nature are our own natural cycles, the rhythm of life everywhere is the pulse of our own heartbeat. We are an intrinsic part of her and the connection stretches over aeons to create a common ancestry for all human beings: our spiritual roots are firmly embedded in the Earth. It is by tapping into this timeless knowledge that we unearth our own deep-rooted instinct and contact the inner strength, the healing power, the majestic serenity that is our human heritage.

Earth is the Great Goddess, Gaia, worshipped over millennia by ancient peoples. Everything that exists is born of the Goddess: all the people, all the animals, all the plants, all the stones, all the stars. She is the creative life-force, for without her nothing exists. Since Spirit can only be made manifest in Matter, Female always contains the seed of Male within her, just as Goddess contains God. It is through the Feminine Principle that Existence comes into being, it is through the embodiment of Goddess energy that the creative life force comes into existence. She is the Great Mystery, the Oneness that is the Source of All … She is the creator and the creation.

The Great Goddess is the life-giver, the nurturer, the protector. She is also the death-bringer, the destroyer, the annihilator. She embraces duality, for she knows that transcendence is an acceptance of both polarities of Existence. She is both light and dark, for she holds within her the great cycles of Nature, the constant dance of life and death. She is both good and evil, both Goddess and Devil, for she knows that one cannot exist without the other. She is both young and old, for she holds within her the wheels of time. She is past, present and future: she is change itself. She is both form and formless, for through her everything is and is not, through her everything comes and goes – and returns in an endless spiral of rebirth.

The Great Goddess is the beginning and end, for within her lie all possibilities, the whole of Creation … for she is the One.

Get Real!

'Getting down to earth' means getting down to basics! And getting down to basics means starting at base camp. In other words, we take the first step into the circle with our most basic nature: the body. We take steps with our feet, making contact with the ground beneath us: these are our roots into the Earth. Our physical nature is the most tangible one whilst we walk our path in this life, so it makes sense to get in touch with it before we do anything else! Getting down to earth means getting real – and the most accessible reality is right here, right now in the body! It is no surprise that the first energy centre in the body is the base or root chakra, located at the base of the spine and related to the element of Earth.

This chakra is the foundation of the Sushumna, the central energetic core of the body. It is at this energetic centre that we start to awaken our consciousness: it is the beginning, the first manifestation of life-force or Spirit in the physical body. It is here that the quantity of physical energy that we have available to us can be sensed: this is our will to live, our ability to say 'YES!' to life. It is here that we experience being fully in the body, or embodiment: this is our ability to say 'I exist, I am here!' This is the energy of One, the experience of our individuality.

The first chakra is the foundation of our physical, emotional and mental health. It gives us our sense of stability and sanity, our sense of being grounded, of being here now. When there is not enough energy flowing through this chakra, we are poorly, we suffer from frequent physical health problems, we feel low in energy and lack zest for life. In an urban environment, our connection with the Earth element is restricted: we walk on tarmac, we wear rubber-soled shoes, rarely are we in direct contact with Nature. The rise in recent years of chronic fatigue syndrome and the increasing frequency of minor infectious diseases most of us suffer from, is surely a sign of weak Earth energy.

When our Earth centre is closed to the life-force of creation, we feel unsupported by the world, as if the very ground we stand on is about to be pulled away from under our feet, as if Existence has abandoned us to the random whims of fate. We feel spaced out, disconnected, unable to get it together. When the energy of Earth is not readily available to us, we have difficulty getting things done and are unable to manifest our dreams. I frequently meet people who complain of these feelings, or who are always dreaming up great plans but never putting them into action: there's always some excuse as to why life has conspired to prevent things happening. I say to these people: **'Stop dreaming, stop thinking, get your head out of the clouds and get down to Earth! Start getting in touch with your body ... feel your feet on the ground beneath you!'**

I, too, was one of these dreamers. I could fabricate the most detailed, grandiose and wonderful future for myself in my imagination, but somehow it was always a rainbow I chased: 'one day' I would be rich, 'one day' I would have this, do that, etc, etc. It was only when I listened closely to my body that I started to manifest my desires. It was only when I looked closely at my reality on a day-to-day level that I could even take the first step towards these dreams.

The base chakra is related to the feet, legs, rectum, spine and the immune system. When this energy centre is open, we literally draw energy up from

205

the Earth beneath us through our feet, up our legs, into the perineum – that bit between your anus and your sex centre – and up through the base of the spine or coccyx. Just like the roots of a tree drawing nourishment from the soil of the Earth, we also take in sustenance from the life-force of the planet. If this flow of energy is too weak, then we too become weak and ineffective, unable to stand up for ourselves, spineless and unable to have a firm hold on life. In some people, there is a vast quantity of Earth-energy available, but it is stuck at the level of the first chakra, unable to flow freely upwards through the spine. And so, in these people, there is an obsession with organization, a rigidity of attitude that gives little room for something new to take root, and unwillingness to budge for fear of having to let go.

When Earth energy is stuck at this first level, there is a strong desire for the security of permanence (although of course this is illusory, as everything changes!). When Earth energy is stuck, there is an over-attachment to the material realm, an over-reliance on time and money as the source of well-being. Again, our urban world encourages this attitude: lack of movement on all levels of being just exacerbates stuck energy. When we are not physically active enough, when we do not get out into Nature, when we do not breathe fully, when we do not express our emotions, when we do not find time for silence, when we have lost our connection with the spiritual dimension of life … all this simply keeps energy stuck at the first gate, the first doorway to higher consciousness.

● ●

Try this exercise to bring awareness to your base chakra.

Getting in Touch with Earth Energy

Stand upright with your feet hip-width apart, knees soft (in other words, very slightly bent), arms loosely by your side.

Take a deep breath and on the out-breath focus on relaxing the muscles around your anus and genitals as much as possible. Just become aware of the sensations around this area for a few moments.

Now lock your knees and squeeze your buttocks together – become aware of how you are feeling right now.

Now once more take a deep breath, soften the knees and relax the muscles of the perineum (anus and genitals) – become aware of how you are feeling.

This exercise shows you how it feels when the base chakra is open and closed. By softening the knees, you facilitate the flow of Earth energy upwards, and by keeping the perineal muscles relaxed, you open the energetic centre of the first chakra. With practice and awareness, you should start to feel a warmth or tingling in this area ... go on, you might as well enjoy it! You may also feel somehow safe and at ease with everything. This is Earth-energy flowing through the first level (later you can learn to draw this energy upwards to the next level). By contrast, when you make your legs rigid, you block the life-force from rising, and by clenching your buttocks, you close the base chakra. You may notice how there is no pleasant sensation here now and how this may make you feel rather uptight and on edge, somewhat afraid and alone. Next time you're standing in that queue at the checkout, just

207

soften your knees, relax your butt and breathe ... everything will be just fine!

● ●

Whether there is not enough energy available or whether there is too much with nowhere to go, a disturbance in the flow results in a fear-based stance to life. On the other hand, when Earth energy is flowing healthily upwards, then we feel nourished, supported, there is always enough. When we are connected to the abundance of the Earth, then we can tap into the wealth of our inner being. Earth energy is the seed within us, whether this be our ability to give life to another human being or our capacity to initiate new projects. And with this energy, just like a tree that bears fruit in time, we have the strength and wisdom to bring our creative ideas to fruition.

When we are connected to the timeless wisdom of the Earth, then we are in tune with the cycles of Nature and with our own inner cycles. Even man-made constructs, such as the political 'tide' and the economic 'climate', are subject to a rhythmical pattern. When we are attuned to this rhythm, then we are in touch with the true source of our nourishment and our life-force flows abundantly.

With the advent of 'civilization', we have increasingly cut ourselves off from our roots and so our foundations for the future are shaky. The rise in global violence, stress-related disease and ecological disaster is testimony to our disconnection from Mother Earth. We have forgotten that there is only one source of life and that we all stem from this source. Our roots go deep, through brothers and sisters, mothers and fathers, generations and ancestors, and even deeper through primates, mammals, reptiles and single-celled organisms. The Tree of Life extends in all directions to include all living creatures, plants and minerals. Consciousness resides everywhere in one form or another … indeed, We Are All One.

The energy of 'One' is not only the first manifestation of Spirit, but also our first connection with something greater than ourselves: this is the energy of **tribal power**. We all have a need to be a part of a tribe, a need to be a part of the whole. We first learn about tribal power from our families: this gives us our sense of belonging, a group identity. Here, we learn about living together, sharing together, growing together. As we grow beyond our families, we learn how to work, play and create with others. This tribal energy teaches us about bonding, loyalty, justice and honour. Without these values, there would be no friendships and no co-operation; neither would there be any lawfulness or integrity. In other words, there would be no community.

Where tribal power is weakened, we see a breakdown in the cohesiveness of community life. Where there is a disruption in the natural harmony of the Earth, as in the modern technological world, we see a rise in alienation, nihilism and violence. Without tribal values to create a common ground, we are uprooted and alone. When we lose contact with our tribal bonds, we live in fear and separation, fighting for survival amongst a sea of strangers.

With the breakdown in the communal family model and, more recently, with the breakdown of the nuclear family, we are increasingly searching elsewhere for common values. Perhaps you find this by supporting a particular football team – you can positively feel the tribal power that is generated when football fans get together! Or perhaps you are an ardent follower of the Gabrielle Roth 5Rhythms movement, going to several classes a week, monthly workshops, yearly retreats, meeting the same people and being part of the ever-growing 'dancing tribe'.

Movements of any kind are always fuelled by tribal energy. In particular, youth-culture and counter-culture movements are strong anti-establishment statements. Rockers, punks, hippies, ravers ... these are all modern-day tribes. Today, there are tribes within tribes, each defined by what music they listen to, what they wear, where they hang out and whom they meet. Admission to a tribe might not even be so dependent on such an extensive list of details. Just being 'alternative' as opposed to 'mainstream' already creates a division of tribes: there is a sense of belonging that comes with being classified as either one or the other.

Tribal power is a double-edged sword, however. This is where we inherit both our **ancestral burdens** and our **ancestral blessings**. Earth energy may become stuck and so the tribal values that we learn become limiting factors. Family conditioning, group belief systems and cultural attitudes can all hold us back from living our full potential. If Earth energy is not flowing through us, then we can cling to values that no longer serve us. For example, you may have inherited the belief from your family that 'I must work hard to survive' or you may have inherited the Judeo-Christian belief that 'God will punish me for doing something wrong'. These are commonly passed down values in our Western society, even though they are mostly unconscious. Even being anti-establishment or alternative can be a limitation, for this is perpetuating the illusion of right–wrong, good–bad, the illusion of duality.

When taken to an extreme, such polarization of value systems leads to warfare, whether this be the gang warfare of inner city slums or whether it be the fanatic terrorism of fundamentalist religious groups.

The challenge is to bring limiting tribal bonds to consciousness and to choose to break these patterns whilst still maintaining the basic tribal values of bonding, loyalty, justice and honour. The challenge is to extend your tribe to the whole world, to honour yourself and to honour other people. Perhaps the Rainbow Family Tribe comes closest to demonstrating this principle: these are people from all over the world who have been coming together every year since 1972 in huge gatherings to dance, sing, make music, discuss, heal, barter and share. These are urban people who care for the environment, care for the future and care for each other. Anybody can take part and there is no membership other than an open heart. There are a number of Hopi prophecies that talk of the emergence of the Rainbow Family. One of them goes like this: 'You will see many youth, who wear their hair long like my people, come and join the tribal nations, to learn their ways and wisdom ...' With the resurgence of dance culture, Earth-centred wisdom and Shamanism in the urban world, it seems that more and more people are joining this family.

● ●

This visualization exercise will help you to connect with the element of Earth by bringing your awareness to the base chakra – it provides the foundation for awakening Earth energy.

Welcoming Earth into Your Body

Sit upright, either cross-legged or in a straight-backed chair. Close your eyes and take a few deep breaths, relaxing your body. Take a few moments to get a sense of how your body is making contact with the ground beneath you, the pressure of your sitting bones, your thighs, calves, feet. Keep your breath relaxed and natural.

Now move your attention to the base of your spine – take some time in getting a sense of how your body is resting here, how gravity is anchoring you from this point into the Earth. This is your foundation, the starting point of the Sushumna. Now align the rest of your body over this anchor, imagining a central column of energy rising upwards, starting with the lower belly, then the middle abdomen, the chest, the neck and right up to the crown of the head. When you are ready, take a few more deep breaths and take a few moments to allow any excess tension to fall away, staying balanced over your anchor.

Bring your attention once more to the base of the spine and imagine here a ball of red light; as you breathe into this ball of light, imagine it melting like hot lava, the red light spreading through your legs and feet and down into the ground beneath you. Imagine it flowing deep down into the Earth, rivers of red light going down to the very centre of the Earth. And at the centre it joins a huge red ball of red glowing red light, the heart of the Earth. Spend a few moments breathing into this huge pulsating light and then as you breathe in, imagine drawing this red light back up to the base of your spine. And with each breath, draw it higher until it starts to radiate throughout your body, feeling the warm glow spread.

When you are filled with red light, come back to the anchor point, take a few deep breaths and allow any excess energy to drain away back into the Earth. Now very gently allow your body to sway slightly – back to front and side to side – all the while staying anchored at the base. Notice how there is always a point of stillness within the movement – this is your base chakra.

● ●

● ●

These simple physical exercises will specifically awaken Earth energy by directly working on the base chakra.

Earth Awakeners!

1. SQUEEZE IT!

Sit cross-legged with your spine aligned.

As you inhale, squeeze the muscles of the perineum (anus and genitals); hold for a few seconds and release on the out-breath.

Repeat a few times.

ROCK IT

2. ROCK IT!

Sit on your heels with your hands on your thighs.

Take a deep breath in through the nose as you rock your pelvis back and then breathe out as you rock your pelvis forwards.

Repeat a few times.

breathe in
and bend

breathe out
and straighten

rock pelvis
back and forth

bend and
rock pelvis

ROCK IT SOME MORE!

3. ROCK IT SOME MORE!

Stand with your feet wider than shoulder-width apart, knees slightly bent and feet slightly pointed out.

Take a deep breath in and bend your knees as far as you can, then come up on the out-breath. Repeat a few times.

Standing in the original position, take a deep breath in and rock your pelvis back and forwards on the out-breath. Repeat a few times.

Combine the above two movements, so that as you bend your knees up and down, you are also rocking your pelvis – remember to breathe! Repeat a few times.

In all these exercises, you should start to feel a warm energy around your perineum – you may even feel it rising upwards as a rush or warm flush. The more you focus your total attention on this area whilst staying relaxed, the more you will feel the energy.

● ●

● ●

This is a grounding exercise – it connects you to the Earth element by making strong contact with the ground through your feet and legs. It also starts to draw Earth-energy upwards through the root chakra and up the spine to awaken the higher centres.

HOO!

Stand with feet shoulder-width apart, raise your arms slightly above
your head and now jump up and down, making sure you keep the
feet flat, the knees soft and the rest of the body as relaxed as possible.

As you make contact with the ground, make the sound 'Hoo!' on the
out-breath, letting it emanate from deep within – if you can imagine
the sound coming from the base of the spine, all the better. Keep the

muscles around the anus and genitals relaxed, as this will keep the base chakra open and enable energy to flow freely.

Continue for as long as possible – at least a few minutes. If your legs start to vibrate, this is a good sign – Earth energy is moving upwards.

● ●

● ●

Now you can put on some music and 'get down to Earth!'.

I Am Here!

Stand with your feet firmly planted on the ground, knees soft and rest of body relaxed.

Take a few deep breaths and then let your awareness drop down to your feet – imagine that all you are is a pair of feet and allow them to move in any way they want. Be in your feet! It is as if your feet are saying, 'I AM HERE!'

Now go through every body part like this, spending a few minutes in each part, in this order: knees, hips, spine, chest, shoulders, arms, hands, neck, head, face. Really BE in each body part, exploring the range of movement, the feelings and sensations, the rhythm ... each body part will be doing its own dance. Each part of the body is saying, 'I AM HERE!' Make sure you keep breathing into the body parts as you move through them. If you find yourself getting back into your head, full of thoughts, spacing out or feeling disconnected from your body, just breathe a little more deeply and bring your awareness back into the part you are working with. Be in your body! Enjoy your physicality, the solidity of your bones and muscles ... enjoy being in your skin ... enjoy your body's unique expression ... enjoy being YOU! You are saying, 'I AM HERE ... I exist ... this is who I AM!'

When I do this in a workshop, we also work together as a group, so I ask each participant to dance with someone else, changing partner's every few minutes. We are saying to each other, 'Here I Am!' It is a practice in being who you are in the presence of another.

● ●

● ●

Now you are ready to dance the Element of Earth. Put on some 'earthy' music, perhaps with some didge sounds and drums, something tribal.

Earth Dance

Stand with your feet firmly planted, the rest of your body relaxed; close your eyes.

Imagine drawing a deep breath up from the Earth beneath you and draw it into your feet. You can add a visualization if you wish: as you draw up the breath, imagine you are also drawing up golden light and let it fill your feet.

Keep drawing up the breath/golden light so it moves up your lower legs and then your upper legs – take your time so that you really feel the glow as you are filled with this subtle energy. And allow your body to move as you do this.

Continue so that this breath/golden light starts to permeate your pelvic area, again allowing the body to move. Keep drawing it up the spine, vertebra by vertebra, so the spine sways and stretches. And continue upwards to your neck and head until you finally reach the crown.

Allow the whole body to be filled with breath/golden light as you move – you have begun to dance the Element of Earth!

Now add the Breath of Fire – and let go!

As you move into trance-dance, keep your awareness in your body – firm feet, strong legs – feel the power of your physical nature, feel the power of your aliveness! Feel the connection with Mother Earth, the strength of her body beneath yours, the creative life-force pulsating deep in her belly. Feel the rhythm of your heartbeat, the blood coursing through your veins, the raw energy of the source. Let yourself go down, deep down into the Earth. Contact your primal nature, feel the animal inside! Lose yourself – become wild like an animal, make sounds from deep within. Earth is both light and dark, both creator and destroyer. Let yourself become the Goddess who is All. Feel the glory of your being – you are Spirit made manifest! Honour your body, embrace your physical nature, express your individuality. Say 'YES!' to who you are in this very moment! Say 'YES!' to life!

Now take a few moments to ground yourself:

Allow your body to slowly come to a standstill, swaying until the energy subsides and a sense of vibrant stillness pervades you.

Once more, become aware of your feet making contact with the ground. Let your roots go deep into the Earth.

Place your hands on your 'sex' and say 'YES!' (quietly or loudly!) to life.

● ●

● ●

Things to Do (or Be) Every Day

- Walk/jog/run!
- DANCE!
- Remember to relax your butt at all times – especially when you are standing!
- When you are sitting, just take a few moments to feel the base of your spine making contact with the solidity of the surface beneath you.
- Walk BAREFOOT whenever you can – on the grass, on wooden floors, on fur rugs ... on anything natural!
- Get out into NATURE as much as possible!
- HUG A TREE!
- Lie on the Earth and let yourself sink in!

- GET YOUR HANDS DIRTY in some soil – plant a tree, some flowers, a window box.
- Say THANK YOU once in a while for the food on your plate, the roof over your head, the clothes that you wear, the circle of people you know, all the beautiful things around you, for the Earth supporting you, for the gift of life!

Chapter 16

Go With the Flow!

He was a holy man who for many years believed only in the river and nothing else. He noticed the river's voice spoke to him. He learned from it; it educated and taught him.

HERMANN HESSE, *Siddhartha*

The Story of Water

Water is the universal womb from which we were born. Water is the source of all life: aeons ago, before the first simple organisms emerged, life was just one big cosmic soup. We are watery beings originating from a watery past. Through lifetimes, we have evolved from sea-dwelling creatures; within a lifetime we evolve from the pre-natal cocoon of amniotic fluid. Water is the blood in our veins, the plasma in our cells, the tears that we shed. Without Water, our bodies would shrivel up into a pile of dust. Water is the rain that falls from the sky, the springs that bubble up from inside the Earth, the rivers that endlessly flow, the seas and oceans that cover most of the planet's surface. Without Water, all life forms would die.

Water is our ancestral record, our collective unconscious. Water holds the blueprint of our experience, haunting us with memories, dreams and reflections. Water is our instinct and intuition, the realm of the feminine.

Water is ruled by the Moon Goddess; for she holds the mysteries of our emotions. She is the Goddess of the Night, the ruler of all that is dark and hidden. Just as the moon waxes and wanes, so do our emotions come and go. Just as the moon exerts a magnetic pull on the Earth's water levels, so do the tides of our feelings rise and fall. She is the Goddess of Death and Rebirth, for when we fully surrender to the depth of our feelings, we die to the 'known' and we are born anew into the 'unknown'. By flowing with our feelings, we are renewed, just as free-flowing water cleanses, purifies and heals. Like gentle rainfall, it refreshes and quenches our thirst. Like a river gushing downstream, it washes away the dirt and heals our wounds. Like the hypnotic lapping of the sea-tide, it quells the pain and soothes our soul. Like a bubbling brook, it brings innocent delight and playfulness. Like a still lake, it brings clarity and peace of mind.

Water is endlessly fascinating, forever shape-shifting, constantly in motion. Moving in circles and spirals, it creates an intricate pattern, a subtle dimension. Like the tide, which ebbs and flows, life follows a rhythmical cycle. If we fight the natural flow, we risk drowning in a sea of turbulent emotions. If we dam up our feelings, we risk being torn apart by the forces of our own repression. By letting go, we stay buoyant and we learn to ride the storm until it passes. By going with the flow, we surf the waves of Existence and stay forever fresh and vital.

Water is holy, it has the power to heal and make whole. It is in water that Christ was baptized to wash away his sins, it is water that we drink to flush away impurities. Water is the river of life, always returning us to Source.

Water is the eternal fountain of youth from which we are reborn over and over again.

Ebb and Flow

Going with the flow means being able to swim with the tide; and the tide always ebbs and flows, there is always movement. Going with the flow means being fluid, flexible, being able to change directions. Changing directions means going forwards or backwards, up or down, left or right, this way or that. Here there is a polarity, a duality: the 'energy of One' has become the 'energy of Two'. This is the energy of the second chakra, related to the element of Water.

This is the sacral chakra, located just beneath the navel, in the belly. Here is the watery womb, here is the source of slippery semen. Here are our reproductive organs, held within the pelvic crucible, just like a cup holding water. Here, in the second energy centre, the raw undifferentiated life-force of the first chakra has divided into two. Here, there is male and female, there is separation and union, there is the attraction of opposites. Here is our ability to come together and procreate, to 'go forth and multiply': this is the power of our sexual energy. Here, we give birth to our offspring, whether these be our children or our creative projects.

When this energy centre is functioning well, our cup is full, we are brimming with creative energy, we are content with our lot and we are centred in ourselves. It is no coincidence that this chakra is the centre of gravity for the physical body; it is also the *hara* or *tan tien* in martial arts, the point of

225

balance or centre of power from which all movement flows. Centredness requires good grounding: in other words, strong roots, feet firmly planted, knees soft, perineum relaxed. In this way Earth energy can flow upwards and collect in the pelvic crucible.

Unfortunately, our urban lifestyle discourages this position because we spend so much time sitting down and have such poor posture habits. Most of us have a habit of holding in our belly. So-called posture correction at school, gym instructors who bark at us to tuck it in, and the obsession with flat tummies in modern culture are all to blame, as is the consistent wearing of high heels by women. All this limits our ability to take a full breath, and so energy gets blocked here and we lose our centredness.

● ●

Try this exercise to get in touch with your sacral chakra.

Getting in Touch with Water Energy

Stand with your feet hip-width apart, knees slightly bent and the rest of the body loose and relaxed. Close your eyes, take a deep breath and, on the exhale, relax the muscles of the anus and genitals.

Now take another deep breath and, on the exhale, bring your attention to your belly, about three finger-widths below your navel.

Now just breathe in and out gently, watching how the breath rises and falls as your belly rises and falls. If it helps, you can softly place a hand here to keep you focused.

Stay aware of any feelings, sensations and emotions that may arise as you breathe here.

● ●

When this centre is weak, then we lack creative impulse, we abort our creations, perhaps starting something and then easily abandoning it. When we are not centred, we remain unfulfilled, always yearning for something but never attaining it. So many people in the modern world are not centred in their *hara*, in their creative power centre. The urban lifestyle of working '9 to 5' in order to earn a living does not allow us to follow our creative urges and so we remain out of synch with our true desires, out of touch with our passion. And so we remain barren; life seems rather dry and empty, we remain unsatisfied; life loses its zest, its juice. This makes us unbalanced as we search blindly for satisfaction wherever we can find it. Drugs, sex, food, addictive relationships, anything to fill up the 'hole' inside – all these are signs of Water energy being out of balance. But rather than making us feel better, they just take us further away from our centre and the cycle of addiction continues.

When Water energy is flowing through us healthily, we are juicy, we are sexy and attractive, we have a certain magnetic pull that draws others towards us. Here is the push and pull of desire, the yearning to merge with another and the need to stay separate. This is the realm of relationship. Here, one has become two, 'I am' has become 'here I am and there you are', 'you and I' become 'we'. Relationship is a dance of polarities. It is here that we experience pleasure and pain, it is here that we learn about the depths of our feelings, it is here that we are buffeted by strong emotions.

227

Relationship always takes us deeper into ourselves, it always reveals our darker side. A relationship is a 'ship' of 'relations': it is here that we act out the unconscious patterns inherited from our family conditioning. And of course, it's a ship ... this is the world of Water, remember?

● ●

This will help you connect with the energy of Water.

Welcoming Water into Your Body

Sit cross-legged or on a straight-backed chair. Close your eyes and take a few moments to ground yourself – become aware of your sitting-bones on the ground beneath you, the weight of your body being pulled down, the base of the spine and how the rest of your body is aligned over this anchor point.

Now get in touch with your breath – just watch how your breath comes and goes as you gently inhale and exhale through the nose. As you continue to focus on your breath, become aware of how it rises and falls within your body, just like a wave rising and falling, like the tide ebbing and flowing. Let your breath go deep in and out of your belly and let yourself be aware of any feelings that may arise as you do this. They may be pleasurable feelings or they may be feelings of discomfort – either way just let them be released with your breath, let them wash through. Imagine your breath as a stream of water, so that each time you exhale, you are letting go of any feelings that have arisen. If anything is particularly uncomfortable or difficult to let go of, imagine this energy being cleansed, dissolved, washed away by the river of water that is your breath. Allow this river of breath to wash right through your whole body, imagine every cell being bathed. You may find that your body starts to sway a little, to create a gentle rhythm as breath ebbs and flows – let yourself be carried by this energy, imagine your whole being is bathed in the cleansing power of breath.

When you feel you have let go of as much as you are going to, allow your breathing to return to normal and any movements in the body to gently come to a standstill. Bring your hands to your sacral area/belly/ *hara* ... and just feel!

● ●

In relationships, we test our boundaries: how far can I lose myself, how much should I let the other person in, do I trust him/her/myself? It is in the second chakra that we sense betrayal, abandonment and abuse: it is here that we feel 'gutted' when someone lets us down. It is also here that we need to learn to trust our 'gut feelings', our intuition, for Water is the world of feelings, sensations and emotions. When we can take some time out from being in our heads, then we sink down into our bellies and get in touch with the subtle current of our feeling nature. Feelings need to flow, energy needs to keep moving, if we are to stay healthy. Just like water needs to keep flowing if it is not to become stagnant and polluted. When feelings are held back, just like water that is dammed up they eventually burst out uncontrollably and we are overwhelmed; we drown in a sea of emotions.

It is also worth remembering that we are, in fact, always in a relationship – whether it be with another person, with our self, with the world or with God.

We do not exist in isolation, we are always responding, reacting, relating to life. We always have feelings about this, that or the other, even though we may not be in touch with them. When the second chakra energy is weak, then we are cut off from our feelings and we relate from a place of insecurity, mistrust, indecisiveness and jealousy: we feel scared and separate. But when this energy is strong, we have an innate trust in ourselves and in the world around us: we feel secure, confident and connected to the pulse of life.

It is the desire to merge with another, to dissolve our boundaries that gives rise to sexuality. The pull towards another human being is the same as the pull towards God. Sexual orgasm is the complete surrender to Source: it is the closest most people will get to a spiritual experience. Sex, death and spirituality are closely linked, since each of them requires a surrender of the small self, a letting go of ego. When second chakra energy is weak, then our ability to have an orgasm is limited: we are frigid and impotent, we have lost our power. And when energy is strong but stuck at this level, we operate from lust and self-gratification. It is only when this energy can flow through us freely and move upwards through the body that we can fully enjoy a full orgasm. When done with awareness, sex becomes a route to higher consciousness: this is the aim of Tantric practices.

Money, too, needs to flow. Money is a current of energy and needs to keep moving. When we hold onto it, saving it for a rainy day, we are coming from a place of fear and lack: we become miserly, stingy, dried up. Our relationship to money is a reflection of our relationship to everything else. Frequently, people with money issues will have physical problems with their reproductive systems, such as prostate cancer and ovarian cysts. Money, sex and power are the three biggies that our culture is obsessed with – and it is no surprise that these are all related to the second chakra.

It is also no surprise that our attitude to these is off-centre when the modern world is out of balance with natural forces. In our society, we tend to veer from one extreme to the other. Either sex, money and power are seen as dirty, something to be hushed and rejected; we are made to feel guilty if we admit to having a desire for any of these. Or they are something we strive to get as much as we can of, even if it might mean stepping all over someone else. But neither extreme is healthy. Without awareness, there is the potential for manipulation and abuse. This is the root cause of pornography, prostitution, rape, fraud and theft. Neither rejection nor holding on to these energies is the answer, for all that happens is a violation of boundaries.

● ●

These exercises will awaken the energy of Water.

Water Awakeners!

1. LIE BACK AND THINK OF THE GODDESS!

Lie flat on the floor and relax for a few moments.

Now bend your knees, draw your feet in towards your buttocks, put the soles of your feet together and let your knees drop out to the sides. Make sure your breath is steady and relaxed; keep the breath flowing. Make sure your hips, pelvis and thighs are as relaxed as possible; if there is any tension, take a deep breath into this area and breathe it out.

Stay in this position for a few minutes if possible – if you can do it longer, great – then slowly bring your knees together. Rest and then repeat again.

You may find your legs start to tingle or vibrate – this is just energy moving. The longer you can be in the position, the more you can just relax and surrender, the more energy you will start to feel moving through the pelvis/sacral area. This is a passive pose and although deceptively simple, it is a challenging one for men because it requires an attitude of surrender, of receptivity.

circle hips

2. POLISHING A CYLINDER

Stand with your knees slightly bent, anus and genitals relaxed. Take a deep breath in and on the exhale sink down into your belly and relax.

Very slowly start to circle your hips as if you were polishing the inside of a cylinder; be sure to do this very slowly and with your total attention. Keep your breath flowing. As you continue, you can make the breath a little stronger by inhaling through the nose and exhaling through the mouth, as if you were drawing a circle with the breath.

After a few minutes, change direction with the hips and repeat.

Come to a standstill and let your breath come to rest – just feel the sensations in the pelvis!

3. SHAKE YOUR BUTT!

Stand as before, making sure the muscles of the perineum are relaxed.

Just shake your whole pelvic area – hips, buttocks, lower back, belly – right inside too, in the pelvic crucible. Let the shaking be as chaotic as you can – loosen up!

● ●

Energy needs to keep flowing through the second chakra. This is the sacral chakra and we need to make the energy here sacred. When sex and money are made sacred, that is, when we bring awareness to these, then we are neither powerless nor do we have power over anyone else. When they are made sacred, then we have true power, the power to create and to share our creations. When they are made sacred, we honour ourselves and we honour others: now we can join forces without losing our sense of balance. When we join in a sacred way, then the energy keeps flowing upwards towards higher consciousness.

For me, the energy of the sacral chakra has been the most challenging to master. As a woman, though, (when I finally got it right) it has also been the most rewarding. I believe that the vast majority of people are wounded in this area. A long history of sexual abuse, subjugation and disempowerment, of both women and men, has led to a collective perversion of authentic power and sexuality. Our relationships are a mess because we are still playing out the battle of the sexes, however subtly. As a society, our creations are usually tainted with the need for personal gain at the expense of another. We have not yet learnt how to share, how to keep the energy moving rather than trying to hold onto it. This is the challenge of the second energy centre.

● ●

Now you can put on some music and go with the flow! Choose music that is gentle, hypnotic, rhythmical, perhaps with watery sounds.

Find the Flow
Stand with feet firmly planted, knees soft and body relaxed.

Take a few deep breaths and let your awareness sink down into your belly; breathe in and out here, letting the belly rise and fall.

Now imagine your pelvis as a crucible filled with water and very gently allow the hips to move, all the time taking care not to spill a precious drop of water! Allow the hips to move more and more so that you are making circular patterns; keep the movement continuous and flowing.

Slowly let your feet take steps forward, all the time staying centred in your belly, so that the whole body is flowing, one continuous motion. Keep breathing, keep moving from your centre!

When I do this in a workshop, I ask the group to move around the room and keep flowing from one person to the next, making sure that they breathe and move from their centre together. This keeps the energy flowing round the room and creates a beautiful watery motion as everyone weaves in and out of each other. I call this 'surfing the wave'.

● ●

● ●

Now you are ready to dance the element of Water. Put on some music, again something flowing but it can be quite chaotic too.

Wave Dance

Stand as before and let your breath drop to your belly; breathe in and out here in a long, continuous cycle.

Imagine your breath is like Water, washing in and out of your belly, like the tide ebbing and flowing. Allow this wave-like motion to fill up your whole body, so that you too become like liquid; you melt and merge with the element of Water.

Now add the Breath of Fire and let go!

As you move into trance-dance, let your body become like liquid, swirling and swaying in continuous smooth patterns. Become like a wave on the ocean, surrendering to the power of Water, ebbing and flowing, rising and falling, moving in circles and spirals. And, just like Water, the flow is sometimes very gentle and light, sometimes strong and chaotic. Let yourself sink deep inside, contacting the place of dreams and symbols, the place of intuition and gut feelings – just follow the flow, no need to control or hold onto anything. Allow your emotions to wash through you, cleansing and refreshing your very being. Surrender to the power of the Goddess of the Sea. You are not in control, let yourself be taken by the flow of life. You cannot stop it, it is a powerful natural force. Your whole body has melted, become liquid, no edges, just circles and spirals – just like Water.

Now take a few moments for grounding:

Allow the wave-like motion to slowly subside until you come to a standstill, keeping your eyes closed.

When you are at rest, gently place your hands on your belly – left hand over the right – and just watch your breath rise and fall here. Feel the softness and warmth here and give thanks for the nurturing qualities of the Womb of Life (even if you are a man!).

● ●

● ●

Things to Do (or Be) Every Day

- Drink lots of water (bottled or filtered is best)!
- Have regular baths and showers!
- SWIM (preferably in the sea)!
- Go to the sea-side and just watch the waves.

- Sit by a river/stream/waterfall and just watch the water flowing.
- Meditate on the full moon. Sit in silence, or if you feel like you can do a little ritual. Go deep into your belly and get in touch with what it is you want to let go of in life, and then just imagine it being washed away.
- Dance under a full moon!
- Get into belly-dancing/salsa/some kind of dance that ignites your passion/eroticism/involves hip-wiggling!
- Make passionate love!
- Make sex sacred. See it as an act of beauty, see it as the force of creation. Do whatever you have to do to make it feel good. Honour yourself and your partner. Try breathing together and take your time letting the energy build up. Check out some books on Tantric practices!
- Clean up you finances! Tidy up any debts, keep clear accounts, and give some cash away!
- BE RECEPTIVE. Go with the flow of life, be open to what life has to offer and follow the path that feels good – you don't always have to be in control!

● ●

Chapter 17

Fire Up Your Power!

> *Every human being is a spark that wants to burst into flame.*

RESHAD FIELD

The Story of Fire

Fire is the flame of awakening: it has the power to awaken consciousness, to enlighten us. Fire gives light so that we may see our way in the darkness, Fire brightens up our day, puts a smile on our face. Fire gives heat to warm our cold bones, Fire melts a frozen heart, makes us feel alive.

Fire is life-giving: without that great fireball in the sky, the Sun, there would be no life on Earth. It is sunlight that helped the first micro-organisms come together in the primordial soup. It is sunlight that provides the energy for the process of photosynthesis so that plants may grow. Fire is transformative. It can change the molecular structure of any substance; it can turn solids into liquids and liquids into gases, it is the necessary trigger for creating a new compound. The alchemists called Fire the 'agent of transmutation': it is a catalyst for change on both a chemical level and, symbolically, on a psychological level, for it is only by feeling burning desire and intense frustration that we are spurred on to change our lives. Fire is purifying. Like a blazing forest fire, which consumes everything in its path, it cleanses by the process of annihilation and thus offers hope of renewal. Like the phoenix rising from the ashes, it is by facing our inner limitations and fears that we burn away what hinders us and emerge anew.

The nature of Fire is paradoxical and contrary: it is both form and formless, forever changing and unpredictable, unable to be contained in any one shape or size. From the gentleness of glowing embers to the delicacy of a flickering flame to the ferocity of a roaring inferno, Fire is in constant motion – yet at its centre is a purity and steady stillness. Fire is sacred. From the first flame ignited by prehistoric man to the ancient Greeks who kept a fire burning in the village centre for protection to the Shamans who used it as a visionary tool to prophesy the future, Fire has inspired awe and respect. Fire is a mediator between the physical and metaphysical worlds: it transports us to the realm of Spirit, it crosses the boundary between the seen and unseen. Fire is creative vision, the divine spark within us all.

Like the flame of divine creativity that Prometheus stole from Zeus to give to humankind, Fire is the gift of the Gods.

The Spark of Life

Getting 'all fired up' means sparking your ignition, revving up your engine, putting a tiger in your tank. It means boosting your energy levels and getting ready for action. The element of Fire is your 'get up and go', it is your will power. Here, the energy of 'two' becomes 'three': this is the third energy centre, the solar plexus chakra.

As energy rises from the second chakra, the fluidity and duality of Water becomes the directness and singularity of Fire. From the polarity of the second chakra is born a third factor: action. As feelings rise up, we have to make a choice: 'should I or shouldn't I?' If we are in touch with our gut feelings, then we instinctively know what is right or wrong for us and so we can make a clear decision: 'I will' or 'I will not'. But if we are out of touch with our deeper self, then there will be a conflict, there will be confusion, a split between what we think we ought to do and what we really want to do. When we are unclear as to which choice to make, we experience this as a discomfort in the solar plexus area: indecision and conflict is a 'stomach-churning' sensation.

● ●

Try this exercise to get you in touch with your solar plexus chakra.

Getting in Touch with Fire Energy

Sit upright or stand, taking a few moments to relax the body and get in touch with your breath.

Let your breath come down to your solar plexus, just beneath the diaphragm; just watch as the breath comes and goes here, as the abdomen rises and falls.

You can place one hand here gently and keep breathing and watching. Stay aware of the sensations and feelings that may arise.

You may get a sense of anxiety or stomach jitters – this is OK, just keep breathing and allow the feeling to melt as the warmth of your hand radiates into your body.

● ●

The energy of Fire not only allows us to digest our experiences, to make sense of our world, but it is also involved in our metabolism: it is our digestive fire, the energy required by the body to break down food into easily absorbed particles. When our fire is well stoked, then our digestive system functions optimally, we are well nourished and we radiate good health. Conversely, when our Fire energy is depleted, we are malnourished, sluggish, low in energy and lacking in enthusiasm. This link between processing our food and processing our life experiences is interesting to me because for years I ate a mainly raw diet, believing this to be the ultimate super-diet for well-being (as was the fad in the 1980s). I couldn't understand why I felt so low most of the time – not to mention so bloated! Not only did I experience almost constant discomfort in my stomach, but I also was pretty uncomfortable with myself and my world; nothing was quite right and I never knew what I really wanted. Getting my fire energy going has taken a combination of emotional and dietary changes: I have had to feed the flame of both my digestive mechanism as well as my will power.

● ●

This visualization will help you feel the energy of Fire.

Welcoming Fire into Your Body

Sit upright and ground yourself, feeling your body make contact with ground beneath you, getting in touch with the base of the spine and anchoring the rest of your body above this point.

Bring your attention to the solar plexus, just beneath the diaphragm; breathe gently in and out here.

Imagine there is a small flame right in the centre of your solar plexus and as you breathe here this flame flickers. Feel the warmth gently radiating from this flame. Breathe a little more deeply and allow this flame to grow, to become a ball of fire that starts to radiate out through your body. Imagine the vibrancy of this golden yellow colour and the heat as it spreads right through you. Imagine this is an 'inner Sun' with rays spreading in all directions. Imagine this inner fire burning through any impurities in the body, let it purify any negativity, transforming and healing any pain. Keep going until you feel energized and uplifted.

When you are ready, allow the Sun's rays to return to the centre of your solar plexus and bask in the afterglow!

● ●

Because our 'civilized' culture encourages us to stay cool, to put a lid on things, our Fire is frequently dampened and the emotional charge gets stuck at the third energy centre. And so we get swamped by negative feelings. We get so overwhelmed by the conflict of the decision-making process that we end up backing down, giving up: inertia sets in, we feel depressed and our self-esteem suffers. When our emotions are out of balance in this way, we lose control of ourselves, we lose awareness and start reacting moodily, erratically, childishly.

When we lose our 'get up and go' energy, we frequently search for sustenance elsewhere. We may unconsciously try to emotionally dominate someone close to us, because this makes us feel more powerful, but ultimately this is a sign of weakness. Or we may reach out for stimulants – coffee, cigarettes, alcohol, amphetamines – anything to keep us going, to give us a buzz, to keep ourselves up. Our fast-paced urban lifestyle encourages this attitude. We are expected to work and play hard and so we frequently burn the candle at both ends and end up burning ourselves out! But this artificial stimulation just serves to keep us disempowered, for true strength only comes from within.

When we refuse to listen to our feelings, when we ignore the voice of intuition, when we bottle it all up, then we are out of control. Frequently, all this repressed Fire energy will simply explode in a violent rage, we become hot-headed and quick-tempered. Fire that is out of control is destructive; it burns those closest to it and consumes itself too. Fire energy that is out of control creates toxins in the body and leads to poor health. Fire that is out of control is like the God of War, Mars: he is out to destroy everything in his path.

The element of Fire sits in our solar plexus: this is our inner Sun. And just like the Sun, this energy fills us with warmth, passion and power. When the sun shines, we feel relaxed, at ease, carefree; we can laugh and play. When the sun shines, we radiate warmth and affection to those around us; we are generous and protective. When the sun shines, we have an inner smile that is infectious and attractive. We draw others towards us so that they may bask in our glory, so that they may share in the abundance of our inner wealth. Solar plexus energy is majestic, royal, we are rulers of our own empires, masters of our own creations. We are self-empowered, we have self-esteem, self-respect, self-responsibility. When Fire energy is strong, we can transform the 'worrier', that part of us that is indecisive, to the 'warrior', that part of us that takes action. Fire energy is the hero within, a spiritual warrior whose light of awareness purifies negativity.

● ●

These exercises will awaken the power of Fire within you.

Fire Awakeners!

1. PUMP IT UP!

Sit upright, cross-legged or on a chair. Take a few moments to relax and get in touch with your breath.

Now pull in the muscles of your abdomen very rapidly so that you make a short sharp exhale and just relax on the inhale. Keep doing this and you will find that the inhale happens on its own – a pumping action is created.

Do this, say, 20–30 times (or as long as you can without straining) and then take a long deep inhalation and let the exhale relax on its own.

You can repeat this cycle several times.

You may start to feel an intense warmth arising in the solar plexus – great!

push down

2. YOU ARE THE SUN

Stand upright, feet hip-width apart and arms over your head.

Take a deep breath and stretch up as high as you can with your fingertips.

As you exhale, bring your arms down to your sides slowly, as if you were pushing against an invisible force. Imagine you are the Sun and your arms are the rays, burning away through any obstacles that stand in your way. Imagine there are golden threads of light emanating from your fingertips, creating a circle of fire around you.

Repeat several times, and then come to rest and know you are the centre of your universe!

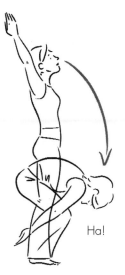

Ha!

3. CHOPPING WOOD!

Stand with your feet slightly wider than your hips and feet firmly planted
on the ground. Keep the knees slightly bent and everything else loose.

Raise your arms above your head with hands clasped, as if you were
holding an axe. Take a deep breath in through your nose and arch
back a little, then as you exhale make the sound 'Ha!' and at the
same time let your hands swing down through your legs, as if chopping
wood. The exhale and the sound should come from your solar plexus
and the top half of your body should be relaxed as you swing down.

Return to the starting position (remember to keep your knees bent at
all times!) and repeat several times. Keep the movements smooth and

the exhale strong. As the energy builds up, the sound should get louder and more forceful.

Continue for a few minutes and then come back to standing position, place your hands on your solar plexus and breathe deeply.

This exercise, in particular, may awaken intense feelings such as anger. Just keep breathing and watching the energy move. If you really need to you can just go and punch a pillow for a while!

● ●

When Fire energy flows freely through the third chakra, we make the right choices, for now we move beyond duality, beyond 'either/or', beyond the many voices of the small self. As energy moves freely upwards, we are aligned to divine will. And what feels absolutely right for us, is always our higher purpose. When we are in balance, our will and God's will are actually one and the same thing. By honouring ourselves, we are honouring God.

● ●

Now you can put on some music and fire up your power! Use music with a fast rhythm, chaotic, tribal ... drum'n'bass is good too!

Feed the Flame

Breathe into your solar plexus. You can do the pump for a few minutes if you want as it helps to build up the energy – fire needs oxygen!

Imagine a small flame here and as you breathe it is getting bigger, flickering and glowing until you feel a warmth.

Imagine this fire spreading throughout your body and let yourself make spontaneous sharp movements with your arms and legs – feet stamping and arms punching. Go faster and faster until the whole body is in chaos – let go into craziness like a child!

When I do this in a workshop, I ask everyone to create a circle in the room. As the energy builds up, one or two people go into the circle at a time and allow themselves to go as wild as they like, the others supporting them by dancing and whooping ... I call this the 'Ring of Fire'.

● ●

● ●

Now you are ready to dance the element of Fire; use music, as before.

Fire Dance

Start with 'feeding the flame', as before. Let the energy build up so that you are consumed by Fire.

Now add the Breath of Fire and let go!

Allow the heat of Fire energy to spread right through you – feel the fire burn! Feel the fire burning through all impurities; let yourself go wild. You are the Destroyer, totally chaotic – nothing to hold onto now, nothing to hold you back! You are the Sun, rays extending outwards, all-powerful, magnificent, huge – you take up all the space. Let the Fire inside explode, like fireworks – a thousand pieces radiating outwards! Dance yourself into oblivion ... you do not exist any more ... melt into nothingness ... you are totally consumed!

When you feel that you have exhausted your Fire energy, that you have come to a place of catharsis, that you are cleaned out, then just allow the energy to settle and come to a standstill.

Now you can ground yourself:

Stay standing and raise your arms above your head. Now slowly bring them down to your side, like the rays of the Sun.

Bring your hands to your solar plexus and bask in the warmth there – this is your inner Sun – smile!

● ●

● ●

Things to Do (or Be) Every Day

- Eat warm/hot food and drink (warm water is always better than ice-cold).
- Light a fire (indoors or outdoors).
- Light lots of candles.

- Sit in silence in front of a candle, eyes soft-focus and just gaze into the flame.
- Bask in the sun (but use a sunscreen!)
- Take off your glasses/lenses, if you wear them, and let the light of day enter your eyes!
- BE WILD AND PLAYFUL!
- Learn to say 'NO!' (once in a while!)
- Release your anger!
- LAUGH a lot!

● ●

Chapter 18

Grow Wings and Fly!

When love beckons to you follow him,
Though his ways are hard and steep.
And when his wings enfold you to him,
Though the sword hidden among his pinions may wound
*   you.*
And when he speaks to you believe in him,
Though his voice may shatter your dreams as the north
*   wind lays waste the garden.*

KHALIL GIBRAN, *The Prophet*

The Story of Air

Air is universal breath, the vital force of creation. Air is invisible yet all-pervading, intangible yet full of secret promise. Air is seemingly invisible, yet it holds the key to life.

Air is made up of the finest etheric energy, vibrating at the most subtle level. This is the domain of the winged ones, of the ethereal sylphs whose gossamer wings cause our hearts to flutter with delight and of the angels whose sweet whispers uplift our souls. Air is the realm of love, where Eros rests until he aims his arrow at your heart, piercing it wide open to reveal the agony and ecstasy of desire – does love not sometimes hurt? Air is the realm of light, where the heart grows wings and is released from the cage of darkness to experience the bitter-sweet melody of joy – is lightness of being not sometimes too much to bear?

Air is the realm of universal mind, of abstract thought and intuitive connections reaching into infinity. The spirit of Air brings stillness and clarity to the mind, elevating consciousness until it shines with crystalline purity like a cloudless sky on a perfect day. This is the domain of our feathered friends, the birds, who with their keen perception and breadth of vision can show us how to soar to new heights. These are the carriers of messages, who, like Hermes the messenger of the Gods, are kept busy to-ing and fro-ing between the celestial and mortal worlds. Air is the realm of sky – and just as a gust of wind can pick up out of apparent stillness, so can the mind make flashes of brilliant insight, which seemingly come from nowhere. This is the realm of inspiration and aspiration; and just as a brisk breeze can blow away accumulated debris, so can the winds of time sweep away the cobwebs of the mind to bring a fresh perspective. This is the realm of change and movement; and so can air inexplicably whip itself up into a frenzy becoming a hurricane, which unleashes its fury until it depletes itself and stops dead just as suddenly as it started. This is the realm of shifting moods and unexpected upheaval.

Air is the realm of Freedom.

The Heart is the Centre

To grow wings and fly means to break out of restriction, to let go of limitation, to relax a little, chill out a little – to lighten up. To lighten up means to stop mooching around with your eyes glued to the floor, to stop dragging your feet as if they weighed a ton. To lighten up means to lift up your head and look to the heavens for a change, to expand your horizons and see life from a higher perspective. Here, there is a sense of space and freedom, you can finally take a deep breath and fill your lungs with fresh air – whew, what a relief!

This is the element of Air and of course it is related to the heart chakra, which also includes the lungs and whole cardiovascular system. This is the fourth energy centre and, as you can imagine, the number four relates to balance and harmony. The number four relates to the four cardinal points on the circle of life, the four elements of the sacred dance of life. And so it is that the heart chakra deals with the balance between the upper and lower realms, the mind and body, and the balance between inner and outer worlds, how we respond to our own private thoughts and needs.

● ●

Try this exercise to bring awareness to your heart centre.

Getting in Touch with Air Energy

Sit upright and take a few moments to relax the body and get in touch with the breath.

Bring your awareness to the centre of your chest and watch how the breath comes and goes here, how the chest rises and falls ... you can gently place a hand here and just stay aware of any feelings and sensations that may arise.

Now bring your awareness to your ribcage: first the front ribs, and let your breath touch them as they expand. Do the same for the back ribs and the side ribs in turn.

You may find as you breathe into your ribcage that some areas feel tight and tense with little movement. You may actually experience the chest cavity as a cage holding you in and you may get a sense that something wants to burst free – just breathe and watch staying aware of the feelings. You may find that after a few minutes the ribs seem to soften and the chest opens up, freeing the breath.

● ●

It is in the heart that all the experiences and feelings generated by the lower chakras accumulate and create our personal myth of suffering and redemption. It is the heart that holds onto old hurt, it is the heart that is wounded in the battle of relationships, it is the heart that hardens with bitterness and regret, it is the heart that becomes ice-cold when love is not there. The heart is the home of the inner child, the vulnerable, sensitive, delicate part of us that was not heard, not seen, not loved. When our heart closes because we can bear the pain no longer, we live in fear, shutting ourselves off from others and ending up aloof and alone.

● ●

This visualization will help you get more in touch with the energy of
the heart.

Welcoming Heart Energy into Your Body

Sit upright, taking a few moments to align your central core, the
Sushumna, over the anchor point at the base of the spine.

Bring your awareness to the centre of your chest, watching the breath
come and go as the chest rises and falls.

Bring your awareness to your heartbeat, an endless pulse that keeps
you alive – just like love, the rhythm is eternal. Keep focusing on this
heart centre and imagine the heart as a flower with the petals gently
folded in. As you breathe here, imagine these petals unfolding slowly,
the sweet fragrance of love spreading out through your body ... stay
aware of the sensations and feelings in your body as you do this. As
you keep breathing and opening the heart, you may feel a range of
emotions, from joy to pain and from peace to vulnerability ... just
allow these feelings to radiate out from the heart and down your arms
into your hands. You may get a sense of longing, a sense that you want
to reach out ... what is it that you yearn for? You can reach out with
your hands in front of you and imagine you are taking whatever it is
that you wish for and bring it your heart. Let your hands rest here for a
while and feel the glow as your heart's desire is manifested in your
body.

When we close our heart to the world, we also close our heart to ourselves, for a closed heart does not allow energy to flow upwards from the lower chakras: a hardened heart cannot possibly be sensitive to the subtle messages of feelings and intuition. And so we cannot take care of our own needs, our own wounded child, we cannot love ourselves. Jesus said: 'Love your neighbour as you love yourself.' In other words, you can only love others as much as you love yourself first. Unfortunately, most of us don't! Loving yourself may seem narcissistic, it may seem selfish, but this concept has been greatly misunderstood in our culture. We tend to gravitate to either one extreme or the other, but you need to remember that the heart is to do with balance.

In our culture, we either completely deny our own needs and try to tend to others – these are the Christian do-gooders, the 'loving' wives, the martyrs who love beating up on themselves – or else we are stuck in our wounding. The current generation of 'thirty-to-forty-somethings', in particular, loves to play 'poor me'. This is the generation of therapy-addicts, workshop-junkies, 'survivors anonymous', etc. Although this airing of wounds, this bringing it all out into the open, this sharing our pain, is absolutely vital for healing, there is a point when you simply have to let go and move on. A wound is a wound and will always be there, you cannot take it away once it has happened. But you can give it time and care so that it heals over and forms a scar. Then it is time to let go. To keep poking at it will just perpetuate the sore.

Letting go of our wounds is the ultimate lesson of the fourth chakra: this is forgiveness, the ability to move on. Forgiveness does not make the wounding right, it does not justify the lack of love: no, it was wrong to be abused, to be violated, to be disempowered like that! To know this is to honour the self, to make proper use of third chakra energy. But at some point you need to say, 'It was wrong and I was hurt, but now I can move on.' Holding on only serves to keep the heart closed: healing happens only when the heart can open again. Remember, however painful it may seem, a heart can never be broken: it can only be opened wider. When it opens wider, then you have the ability to feel the breadth of feelings that are humankind's heritage, the full glory of human suffering and human joy.

Forgiveness is not the same as forgetting. For*getting* is repression, it is holding on, it is *getting* stuck. For*giving*, on the other hand, is being fully aware of the hurt and then releasing it, *giving* it away. This is compassion, this is unconditional love – this is the real lesson of the heart. Compassion means acceptance of 'what is'. It is the ability to hold both extremes at the same time, to experience both suffering and joy, to feel the pain as well as to stay open to love. It is a vulnerable position, but there is great strength here: the more we can embrace 'what is', the bigger we grow. It is a state of balance, of equilibrium: this is the equanimity talked of in Buddhism and it is the goal of meditation.

When the heart centre is open, we have the ability to give and receive, to reach out and draw in. The arms and hands are extensions of the heart centre, they are like wings that extend from the middle of the spine. With our wings we can touch and be touched, we can give and receive love. With our arms and hands, we can hold a baby close to our breast, tenderly caress our lover's hair, gently stroke our pet's head, we can fix something that is broken, wipe away our tears, make a cup of tea and make our world beautiful. With our arms and hands we can also hold on so tight that we strangle the life out of something, we can clench our fists so tight that the blood stops flowing, we can inflict pain and we can make a mess. The hands are extremely sensitive and expressive instruments, just as the heart is a sensitive expression of our soul.

● ●

These exercises will start to awaken Air energy within you.

Air Awakeners

1. GROW WINGS!

Stand with feet firm, knees soft and body relaxed.

Bring your awareness to the centre of your upper back, between the shoulder blades and breathe deeply here.

Imagine you have wings that sprout from this point and as you breathe they are unfurling. Make circles with your shoulder blades and your shoulders, freeing up any tension here; keep breathing deeply.

Keep making circles and now use your arms as well, stretching them out like wings; extend them outwards and imagine you are flying!

2. FINGER TINGLE

Stand as before, arms loose and by your sides.

Open and close your hands tightly and quickly, making fists several times.

Now shake your hands vigorously for a minute or two.

Bring your hands about 6 inches to 1 foot away from each other, keeping them soft – feel the tingle!

3. WINDMILL

Stand with feet hip-width apart, knees soft and body relaxed.

Bring your arms up and out to your sides, at chest level, and rotate your torso side to side a few times.

Keeping your arms loose, bend forwards so that they rotate lower and then move them up higher, creating a spiral around the torso. Repeat a few times.

Come to a standstill and let the arms rest by your sides.

You may get a sense of lightness and freedom now, especially in the upper body.

● ●

The heart is literally the centre around which our life revolves: it is the pump of life, transporting vital oxygen/*prana*/*chi* to the rest of the body. When the heart stops beating, then our life comes to an end. When the heart centre is open and the breathing is unrestricted, then energy is free to flow upwards, expanding the mind and rising above petty thoughts and worries. In this place of spaciousness and peace, all is well and you are at One. When you are balanced in your heart, you can walk with your head held high and your feet firmly on the ground, you are able to face life as it comes, able to embrace Existence in its totality ... this is the path of Tantra, the path of the mystic, the path of the heart.

My initiation into this path happened a number of years ago when I took part in a *sannyas* ceremony in India. For me, there was no doctrine to follow, no guru, nothing to do ... other than to take a vow – to myself – to follow the path of the heart, to surrender to love, to embrace life fully. This very simple act, this intention, has been a great lesson. It has taken me deeper into myself and has not been easy, for I have had to face suffering in order to open to compassion. All my focus on love and light up until then paled in comparison to the real lessons of the heart – but it has been worth it! Without a heart opening, life is only half-lived!

The heart is the halfway point in the body's energy system, the place of balance. When you are balanced in your heart, you have a sense of direction, a sense of purpose ... and this always leads you to your highest truth, your soul's destiny.

● ●

Now you can put on some music and grow wings and fly! Use music that is light and airy, perhaps with strings and flutes.

Fly Like a Bird in the Sky

Breathe into the centre of your chest, fully expanding your ribs.

Imagine there is a thread of light emanating from the centre of your chest and extending outwards and upwards into the sky. Allow yourself to move from this centre, floating lightly on your feet.

Spread your wings, extending your arms and hands, just like a bird about to take flight – let yourself fly!

When I do this in a workshop, I ask everyone to find a partner and dance heart to heart, imagining there is a cord of light that connects them from their hearts. It is very beautiful to watch everyone dancing from the heart – you can feel the subtle sense of expansiveness in the air!

● ●

● ●

Now you are ready to dance the element of Air. Continue with music, as before.

Dance of Freedom

Breathe deeply into the centre of your chest and 'fly like a bird in the sky', as before.

Now add the Breath of Fire and let go!

Let yourself expand into the space around you, becoming finer and finer until you are almost invisible. You are floating upwards, higher and higher, up into the vast expanse of the Sky – let yourself fly! You are free, no restrictions, no limitations, nothing to hold you down. You can see clearly, you have an eagle eye, you penetrate deep into the nature of things, you pierce the veil of illusion. You commune with the Beings of Light ... you are light ... just being, not doing ... everything is soft, subtle, ethereal, beautiful, blissful! This is the element of Air! You move like the wind, forever changing, drifting, sometimes soft, sometimes with force, but always invisible, always bringing clarity and freshness, vibrancy and aliveness!

Now you can ground yourself:

Gently come to a standstill, like the wind at rest.

Place your hands softly over your heart centre and breathe gently.

Imagine your heart as a flower and slowly close the petals. Give yourself a hug and say 'Thank you!'

● ●

● ●

Things to Do (or Be) Every Day

- Stretch your arms once in a while.
- Shake out your hands once in a while.
- Reach out and TOUCH someone you love!
- Stroke a pet!
- Give someone a BIG HUG!
- BE IN YOUR HEART – just drop your awareness down to your heart-centre and imagine you had eyes there. Walk around like this for a while.
- BREATHE!
- Go outdoors and be in the wind – enjoy!
- Say 'thank you' to someone – and mean it!
- LOVE YOURSELF!!

● ●

Chapter 19

Go Inside!

So this is heaven, he thought, and he had to smile at himself. It was hardly respectful to analyse heaven in the very moment that one flies up to enter it.

RICHARD BACH, *Jonathan Livingston Seagull*

This Is Lift Off!

'Going inside' means withdrawing your attention from the external world, it means closing your eyes and turning inwards. It means getting quiet and getting still; it means finding your stillpoint, finding your centre. It means you have completed the journey around the circle of life and now you step inside: now you stand in the centre of your circle.

This is the fifth element, the place of Great Spirit. Through the gateway of the heart, we move into the higher energy-centres. Whereas the lower centres – chakras one to four – deal with our relationship to the outer world or material reality, the higher centres – chakras five to seven – deal with our relationship to the inner world or spiritual reality. The heart centre actually deals with both the inner and the outer as it is the transition place, but I have included it as a lower chakra because we are still dealing with personal issues here. It is only when energy moves freely through the heart that the higher centres can be reached.

When the heart opens and lightens up, when it can grow wings and fly, then we can take the next step into inner space. Now we move from the seen to the unseen worlds, from the known to the unknown dimensions. This is the edge between form and formless, this is quantum reality, the place of new possibilities. Here, we leave behind the skin-encapsulated ego, we move beyond the small self, we stretch the boundaries of our everyday reality and take a step into the boundless realm of transcendence … this is lift off!

As we step up from the fourth to the fifth energy centre at the throat, we move into quantum space, the element of ether, the place of subtle vibrations, the threshold of Matter and energy. Here is the power of manifestation, the place where thought forms create reality. It is from this place that what we affirm in our thoughts becomes true for us, it is here that what we envision becomes our reality. As we climb higher to the sixth energy centre in the middle of the forehead, our vision expands even more and transcends the limitations of time and space. From this place, we can see more clearly, we can penetrate the deeper reality of Existence. This is the 'third eye', the place of inner vision and insight.

By working with the four elements, by dancing the circle of life, we prepare the way for moving into these higher energy centres – into the centre. Dancing the four elements takes you on a spiral path to the place of transcendence. As you complete the outer circle of life, you take flight into inner space: this is **trance-end-dance**, this is where trance-dance takes over. If you are totally in trance-dance, you will keep flying, you will keep climbing higher, you will keep going deeper inside until you eventually come to the centre, the place of absolute stillness. This is the energy of the seventh chakra at the crown of the head, the place of no mind, the Void, the Source.

Here, there is no separation between inner and outer worlds, you and Existence are one.

Now the circle is complete. You have moved into a state of wholeness, you have moved into One, you have moved into ecstasy!

● ●

These simple exercises help to awaken your inner space.

Let Your Head Roll!
Stand with knees soft, body relaxed, eyes open or closed.

Drop your chin to your chest, let your jaw hang open slightly and slowly roll your head all the way around. If there are any points of tension, just breathe deeply into that area, imagine releasing the tension on the exhale and continue.

Allow any sounds to be made as you roll ('aah!', 'ooh!', whatever ... loosen up the vocal chords!)

Repeat a few times in each direction.

Important: If you have a neck injury, then just do half-circles to the front only.

Look Around!

Stand as before, eyes open.

Roll your eyeballs in a complete circle so that you can see all the way around.

Repeat a few times in each direction.

● ●

● ●

This is a beautiful Sufi exercise – try it! Make sure you have enough room for this, that there is nothing to bump into – outdoors on the grass is great! Get ready to 'go inside'.

Spin into Stillness

Extend your arms to your sides and let yourself spin, slowly at first and then pick up the pace if you can – just like you did when you were a child!

Keep your eyes open, soft-focus and BREATHE! Keep the breath flowing or else you may feel a little sick doing this!

Keep going as long as you like – you can start just doing a few minutes and then build up to 30 if you like! As you settle into a good pace, it will eventually seem as if you are not moving at all – it will feel as if you are totally still at the centre … keep breathing and enjoy!

When you have had enough, just drop to the ground softly with your belly down so that excess energy drains into the Earth. Just lay on your back for a while and then come up to sitting position slowly.

● ●

Now Drop It!

Now all there is to do is **drop it**! To 'drop it' is to completely and utterly let go on all levels – there is absolutely nothing to do but relax! By dropping it you are totally surrendering to Existence. You allow the silence to permeate your being, you give yourself time to stay inside before rushing once more into the outside world. This is **integration**: it allows the energy to settle back down from the higher centres to the lower ones. In other words, it allows consciousness to drift back down into the body. If you do not give yourself the time for integration, you will remain spaced out, ungrounded, unable to interface with the everyday world. This does not serve to enhance your consciousness: it simply keeps it 'out there somewhere' and makes you feel alienated. We grow in awareness by bringing consciousness into the body. Integration means that we make sense of the insights we have made, we increase our self-knowledge and so we grow in wisdom.

Dropping it also means that any excess energy that has been generated and cannot be contained within the body-mind system, (when our vessel is as full as it's going to get) can drain away back into the Earth. When excess energy has nowhere to go, it can cause an imbalance, such as a headache, dizziness or nausea. By allowing this excess to sink back down through the body and be absorbed into the ground beneath you, it will keep you clear and balanced. It is a little like the lightning conductors on top of tall buildings: their purpose is to channel the energy into the Earth so that it does not create havoc where it is not meant to. The Earth is a great container for anything that is superfluous, that is over-spilling: energy that is not needed elsewhere is held within the body of the Earth and recycled. What is deemed 'waste' is always transformed into 'wealth' by the Earth. It is a little like putting manure in the soil – it helps your garden grow!

● ●

Now there is nothing to do!

Drop It!
Just lie on the ground on your back, eyes closed and DO NOTHING!

● ●

● ●

Things to Do (or Be) Every Day
- Close your eyes for a few minutes – GO INSIDE!
- Be absolutely STILL!
- Create some space and time in your home where you can be totally SILENT!
- Pay attention to your DREAMS – keep a journal if you wish. There is no need to interpret or analyse them, just be aware of them; this enhances your inner vision.

- Create an ALTAR. Find objects that you feel attuned to and that represent the four elements (e.g. stones/crystals for Earth; a bowl of water/flower essences for Water; a candle for Fire; incense/feathers for Air). You can also add pictures, symbols ... whatever turns you on! Create a sacred space for this in your home or garden. Enjoy doing it, be creative!
- DO NOTHING!

Chapter 20

Become Holy

> *This reminds me of that time you tried to drill a hole in your head.*

The Hole in Your Head

To be whole is to be holy. To be whole is to be at One – with yourself, with God/Goddess, with All That Is.

To be whole is to be complete. You have reclaimed the fragmented parts of the self. Now the ego is aware. You can see who you are and you can choose how to be in the world. Now you are awake! Waking up does not mean achieving high mystical states, although this may be part of the journey. Waking up means encompassing all of your selves. To encompass means to contain, to surround: in other words, to create a circle. And what is a circle if not a (w)hole?

To be whole means that there is no separation between you and Source – small mind and big mind are one. Now you can embrace whatever life offers, there is no barrier erected to shut out the world. This is a headless state – you are empty, a void. I like to say: **'Let there be a (w)hole where** your head is!' And where there is a hole, it will be filled. Now the whole of Existence is in you. Your emptiness is full – where there is a hole, there is wholeness. You are One with All That Is. And when you are at One, a great love flows through you: every moment there is love because you embrace every moment. This is a holy state, a truly mystical state: for love's abode is in the heart; and the heart is where the mystic finds his way. It is here in the heart that we find the union of Spirit and Matter, the sacred marriage of Heaven and Earth.

The whole of life is a journey to this space, an intricate dance to help you become hol(e)y!

●　●　●　●　●　●　●　●　●　●　●　●　●　●　●　●　●　●　●　●

This visualization is a wonderful way of closing the circle as well as being very grounding and centring. I use it at the end of my workshops but you can do it anytime, anywhere.

Heaven and Earth

Sit upright, preferably cross-legged, eyes closed, body relaxed.

Bring your awareness to your breath as it rises and falls in the centre of your chest.

Bring your awareness down to the base of your spine. Feel the contact of your body on the ground beneath you, the weight of your body being pulled downwards.

Now let your awareness drop down even further, so that it moves into the ground beneath you. Imagine you have roots like a tree, which grow down through the Earth ... deeper and deeper through the layers of soil and rock ... deeper and deeper until these roots touch the very centre of the Earth. Imagine that here in the centre is a glowing ball of red light – this is the heart of the Mother. Allow your roots to draw nourishment from this centre, just like a tree draws nourishment from the soil. As you breathe in, imagine this red light, glowing and warm, full of life-force, being drawn up through your roots and into the base of your spine. Allow it to permeate your whole body, filling it with warmth, and glow.

Now bring your awareness gently back to the breath rising and falling in the centre of your chest.

Now let your awareness drift upwards to the crown of your head.

Let your awareness move up a little higher into the space above your head. Imagine you have branches like a tree, growing upwards, higher and higher ... get a sense of the spaciousness and emptiness above you. Allow these branches to reach further upwards into the sky and right out into the universe beyond. Imagine these branches touching the furthest stars in the galaxy and as they do so there is a cascade of pure white light, which pours back down your branches just like cosmic rainfall. Allow this light to pour into you through the crown of your head and let it fill up your whole body.

Now bring your awareness gently back to the breath rising and falling in the centre of your chest.

When you are ready, slowly open your eyes.

● ●

● ●

Try this beautiful visualization.

All that Is

Sit upright, close your eyes and relax your body.

Bring your awareness to the centre of your chest, breath rising and falling.

Now imagine that there is a tiny pink bubble right there in the centre of your heart. Each time you breathe out, imagine this pink bubble gets a little bigger, so that it starts to fill up with your breath, like a balloon.

Keep doing this. On the exhale the bubble gets a little bigger, so that it fills up with pink healing light and starts to fill up the whole of your body.

As the bubble gets bigger and bigger, it starts to spread outwards beyond your body, so that you are contained inside it.

As you keep breathing into this bubble, it continues to fill up with pink healing light and love coming from the centre of your heart and radiating out across the room you are in so that everything here is contained within it, all the objects, people, etc. Keep doing this so that the bubble gets bigger and bigger so that it spreads out across the city you are in with all the cars and traffic and people and buildings and out across the country you are in with all the trees and rivers and animals. Keep filling with your breath, with light and love, so that the bubble spreads across the world with all the races, all the creatures, all the deaths and the births, all the suffering and the joy. Keep filling up this bubble until it spreads out beyond the Earth and into the solar system and further out into deep space with all the planets and all the stars and all the other heavenly bodies. And keep going until the pink bubble fills up the whole of the cosmos, the whole of creation, All That Is. Stay here a while!

Now very slowly draw this gigantic pink bubble closer and closer towards you so that All That Is is still contained within it, closer and closer until it sits back inside the Earth, until it sits back inside your home, until it sits back inside your body ... and closer and closer until it sits back inside your heart, still containing All That Is. Stay here a while!

Now very gently place your hands over your heart centre and remember, the heart is where Heaven and Earth meet. You are All That Is!

As you do this, you may encounter discomfort and resistance and many emotions may come up – this is great! It is just energy expanding and will help you grow!

Freedom Is the Dance

The whole of life is a lesson in paradox. The more you lose yourself, the more you find something greater. The more empty you are, the more full is your experience. The more you want to go beyond the mundane, the more you should be here now. And so on, and so on.

To be human is to live in this paradox. To be human is to accept both one's mortality and one's divinity, it is a dance between limitation and vision. Just like Prometheus, who stole fire from the Gods and was then punished by having his liver eternally pecked out, we too are constantly yearning for 'something other'.

The fire that Prometheus stole represents the divine creative spark that makes humankind more than mere animals. It also represents self-knowledge, the realization of our own divinity, the light of consciousness. The punishment that Prometheus is subjected to is the suffering that we encounter in trying to rise above our small nature: the path to self-awareness always involves an element of pain as we encounter our resistances. Ignorance is bliss, as they say! It is the same story as that of the Garden of Eden, where Adam and Eve are forbidden by God to eat the fruit from the Tree of Knowledge, for this would awaken them to their own divine nature … and then where would He be?

Luckily, there is an end to the suffering of Prometheus, for he is eventually freed in return for having to wear a crown of thorns for the rest of time. The crown of thorns is a reminder of his mortal nature. It is a reminder that we cannot live in the light all the time. The more we yearn to escape the nitty-gritty of life, the more we will be chained down by the limitations of our own mind. Freedom is the embracing of both Heaven and Earth!

This has been my greatest lesson and therefore my greatest teaching! It is only by coming down to Earth that I have truly experienced the divine. It is only by fully accepting the moment-to-moment reality of my urban world that I have stepped onto the mystic's path. I say: **'Get out of your head, into your body – and let the dance of transformation (or "trance-formation") begin!'**

Freedom *is* the dance!

THE END
(until the next beginning!)

BOOKS TO READ AND MUSIC TO LISTEN TO

BOOKS

Whilst many books have inspired me and expanded my vision over the years, I suggest here only those that are particularly connected to my work and that I make reference to in this book – enjoy!

CHAPTER 2: GET OUT OF YOUR HEAD

Eckhart Tolle, *The Power of Now*, Hodder & Stoughton, 1999 – simply the best book on 'waking up' (or enlightenment)! Totally accessible, totally empowering and is good common sense!

Douglas Harding, *On Having No Head*, Arkana, 1988 – a great little book to snap you out of your habitual perception of how things are. There's also a great website with lots of articles by Douglas Harding as well as lots of simple but very effective exercises to try; check out 'The Headless Way' at www.headless.org

CHAPTER 3: FREE YOUR MIND

Christina Grof and Stanislav Grof, *The Stormy Search for the Self*, Mandala, 1991 – a profound book about spiritual emergence by the man (and his wife) who put consciousness research at the forefront of science and psychology. Lots of practical guidelines too – very useful if you're currently experiencing 'the dark night of the soul' and need to see a little light!

CHAPTER 4: PREPARE FOR GOD … AND WAIT!

Osho, *Autobiography of a Spiritually Incorrect Mystic*, St. Martin's Press, 2000 – a fascinating insight into the life of this much misunderstood spiritual teacher, as well as full of wisdom for the modern seeker.

CHAPTER 5: EXPAND INTO ECSTASY

Nicholas Saunders, Anja Saunders and Michelle Pauli, *In Search of the Ultimate High*, Rider, 2000 – a highly intelligent look at the use of psychoactives in the spiritual quest, from Shamanic traditions to the culture of today. Unlike most other books on this topic (which are few and far between anyway!), this one is not a 'head-trip' but rather is written with heart as well as insight. Puts it all into perspective somehow!

CHAPTER 6: COME INTO YOUR BODY

Deepak Chopra, *Quantum Healing*, Bantam Books, 1989 – an eminently readable overview of the body-mind link from this eminent guru of holistic health! Great for empowering you to be in your body.

Carolyn Myss, *Anatomy of the Spirit*, Bantam Books, 1997 – this book has sort of become 'the Bible' of spirituality from a medical perspective – strange but it makes sense and it works!

CHAPTER 8: DANCE YOUR PRAYERS

Gabrielle Roth, *Maps to Ecstasy*, Thorsons , 1999 – the first book on the dancing path to wholeness – a classic!

Gabrielle Roth, *Sweat Your Prayers*, Newleaf, 1997 – slightly more autobiographical than the first, Gabrielle's second book weaves a magical journey of inspiration. You can also check out details of her 5Rhythms dance workshops at www.gabrielleroth.com (US-based) and at www.mcauk.com (UK-based).

Frank Natale, *Trance Dance: the Dance of Life*, Element, 1995 – a short but sweet book on trance-dance and its Shamanic roots as well as its relevance for today's culture – the only book specifically on trance-dance that I know of. There is more information at www.trancedance.com and also at www.ecstaticspirit.com (US-based).

CHAPTER 13: DANCE YOUR PRAYERS AND
CHAPTER 14: STEP INTO THE CIRCLE
Leo Rutherford, *Your Shamanic Path*, Piatkus 2001 – a down-to-earth and
very readable journey around the medicine wheel. A very useful map of the
journey of life, making ancient wisdom accessible to today's world. You can
also get information about Leo's UK-based trance-dance workshops at
www.shamanism.co.uk

MUSIC

Music is, of course, an integral part of my work. Many of my workshops
involve live music, incorporating several drums and other instruments, such as
guitar, gongs and more exotic things too. When the music is live like this, the
musicians and I work as a team to sensitively guide the group into trance
and to hold the energy for them so that they feel safe to travel into the
unseen realms. The music is totally spontaneous and so it is very alive, very
in the moment, very fluid and very different each time!

However, it is not always appropriate to work with live music and certainly
not if you are doing this at home! And so I have a wide selection of music
CDs that I use: these are drawn from many sources, mainly world/global
music, ambient/techno, and new age/meditative. In addition, some of the
exercises in this book are adaptations of active meditations, which have
specific music to go with them. You can, of course, use any music you like –
as long as it gets you moving – but here are some of my favourites to get
your feet tapping and juices flowing:

CHAPTER 9: EXPRESS YOURSELF!
'Catharsis': (1st & 2nd tracks) 'Dynamic' (Meditations of Osho), New Earth Records
'Go Crazy!': (1st track) 'Gibberish' (Medits. of Osho), New Earth Records

CHAPTER 12: AWAKEN THE SERPENT
'Shake Her Awake!': (1st track) 'Kundalini' (Meditations of Osho), New Earth Records
'Seven Steps to Heaven': 'Chakra Breathing' (Meditations of Osho), New Earth Records

CHAPTER 13: DANCE YOUR PRAYERS
'Trance-end-dance': 'Shaman's Breath' by Professor Trance & the Energisers, Island Records

CHAPTER 15: GET DOWN TO EARTH!
'I Am Here'/'Earth Dance': 'Feet in the Soil' by James Asher, New Earth Records

CHAPTER 16: GO WITH THE FLOW!
'Find the Flow'/'Wave Dance': 'Sacred Memories of the Future' by Cybertribe, New Earth Records

CHAPTER 17: FIRE UP YOUR POWER!
'Feed the Flame' 'Fire Dance': 'Release' by Afro Celt Sound System, RealWorld

CHAPTER 18: GROW WINGS AND FLY!
'Fly Like a Bird'/'Dance of Freedom': 'Sacred Spirit', Virgin Records

Some of these are available in record stores and the rest are obtainable from Changing Worlds Distribution, who have a very wide selection of world/global/techno/ambient music to choose from at
www.changing-world.com
The Osho Active Meditation CDs are available from New Earth Records at
www.newearthrec.com

Some other CDs that I have found very good for all of the above are:
'Waves' by Gabrielle Roth & the Mirrors, Raven Records as well as anything else by Gabrielle Roth & the Mirrors ... music designed for dancing!
'Party for God' by Be-Attitude, Second Wave Productions.
You can get all of these from www.mcauk.com

In addition, myself and the musicians I work with have created a couple of CDs specifically based on my trance-dance workshops:
'Moving into One' – this is a 'techno-shamanic ritual' with techno-tribal music which takes you on a guided journey through trance-dance and the four elements of the sacred wheel of life as well as a guided meditation at the end. Just put it on and go!
'Ecstasy' – our current version based on a live recording to really get you going! As close to the real thing as you're going to get in your living room! Both of these are available from www.movingcreations.com (and look out for more to come!).

Oriah Mountain Dreamer

The Dance

The sequel to the bestseller The Invitation

Oriah Mountain Dreamer, visionary author of The Invitation, the sensational word of mouth bestseller, has written an inspiring new book. The Dance picks up where The Invitation left off, taking the ideas of The Invitation deeper. Each chapter of this book begins with a line from her new poem The Dance, and explores our ability to open up to the adventure of living, facing love, sorrow and anger and learning all they have to teach us. Oriah Mountain Dreamer explores:

- Relationships – what we get wrong and how to fix them
- Money – what it means and how to enjoy it
- Ways to overcome fear and loneliness
- Humour – how to be happier
- How to find balance and harmony in your life.

Oriah Mountain Dreamer answers each of her insightful questions by taking readers with her on a deeply personal, yet universal and inspiring, journey of the heart.

Cat de Rham and Michele Gill

The Spirit of Yoga

A unique journey through the Eight Limbs of the Yoga Sutras of Patanjali.
A truly beautiful and inspiring journey through the yoga sutras of Patanjali.
In this gorgeous book, professional photographer and yoga teacher Cat De
Rham brings her own personal vision to the yoga sutras in words and
pictures. Written over 2,000 years ago, the yoga sutras are a step-by-step
guide to the attainment of true liberation. There are eight stages or limbs of
this quest: the eight limbs of yoga.

The book is structured around the eight limbs identified in the yoga sutras of
Patanjali as follows:
   Yama: the practice of universal ethical disciplines
   Niyama: the practice of individual disciplines
   Asana: the practice of postures or body exercises to develop agility, balance,
   strength and vitality
   Pranayama: the practice of regulating the breath
   Pratyahara: the practice of mastering the senses
   Dharana: the practice of focusing the mind
   Dhyana: meditation
   Samadhi: union with the Supreme Being

In this thought-provoking book Cat leads you through the eight limbs, from
Yama, the practice of universal ethical disciplines right through to Samadhi,
union with the supreme being, shedding light on their philosophical
background, and sharing personal hints and practical tips on how they
translate into both the practice of yoga and our everyday lives. Along with
her stunning artwork and inspirational quotes Cat shares the insights that she
has gained along her own personal path to fulfilment.

Gabrielle Roth

Maps to Ecstasy

A healing journey for the untamed spirit

New Edition of this inspiring classic which takes you on a powerful shamanic dance journey. Discover how you can explore your whole self – body, soul, heart, mind and spirit – and transform your daily life into sacred art.

Become fully alive with Gabrielle's unique shamanic dance process.

Gabrielle Roth describes her own personal journey from conventional dance to an understanding of the sacred rhythms and life cycles that lead to true enlightenment .

Describing how she awakened her own latent shamanic power through a dynamic mixture of dance, song, meditation, theatre and ritual, Gabrielle goes on to show how shamanic principles can be incorporated by everyone, here and now, even in contemporary urban lives.

Barefoot Doctor

Return of The Urban Warrior

High-Speed Spirituality for People on the Run

An accessible, entertaining and innovative guide to everything you need to know to live well in the fast, furious 21st century, from best-selling author and "modern Taoist sage", The Barefoot Doctor.

Return of the Urban warrior is an accessible, entertaining and innovative guide to everything you need to know to live well in the fast, furious 21st century, from best-selling author and "modern Taoist sage", The Barefoot Doctor. This is the guide to surviving and thriving amidst the growing pressures of modern urban life, and tuning in to the global spirit.

This book enables you to make use of brief moments of free time and use them to maximise your spiritual awareness and well-being. Barefoot Doctor prescribes a broad range of Taoist techniques, comprising new meditations, energy work, affirmations and visualisation skills, breathing methods, prayer formats and physical chi exercises.

The book also contains spiritual advice on universal topics from communication skills to making money, loneliness, friends, escapism, taking risks, health, success and failure, addictions, and much more.